DINOSAUR AMIGURUMI

Justyna Kacprzak

DOVER PUBLICATIONS, INC.
Mineola, New York

Everybody loves dinosaurs, and in this fun crochet book you will come face to face with many different kinds of them—from the horned Triceratops to the flying Pterodactyl! Crochet expert Justyna Kacprzak has created detailed instructions to allow you to create fourteen adorable stuffed animal dinosaurs. Perfect for gift giving, they will be welcomed by crocheters and dinosaur aficionados alike!

Bibliographical Note

Dinosaur Amigurumi is a new work, first published by
Dover Publications, Inc., in 2015.

International Standard Book Number
ISBN-13: 978-0-486-79368-9
ISBN-10: 0-486-79368-0

Manufactured in the United States by Courier Corporation
79368001   2015
www.doverpublications.com

CONTENTS

Gauge (all patterns): 1cm x1cm – 3rounds and 3sts

Abbreviations used:
ch – chain
sc – single crochet
hdc – half double crochet
bb – bobble
FLO – front loops only
BLO – back loops only
sk – skip
hdc3tog – 3 hdc worked together
sc3tog – 3sc worked together
3in1 – 3sc in 1 stitch
4in1 - 4sc in 1 stitch
bobble – yo, insert hook in the next stitch, yo and pull a loop, yo and pull yarn through 2 loops,* yo, insert hook in the same stitch, yo and pull a loop, yo and pull yarn through 2 loops*, repeat from * to * once again, yo and pull yarn through all 3 loops

PICKING UP STITCHES IN A HOLE LEFT WHILE WORKING

Sometimes, while working on a pattern, you'll be leaving holes, where you'll pick up stitches for some body parts (neck and legs sts). It'll look, for example, like this (ch4, sk4):

round x

round y

It is important not to work in chain spaces, but in each chain individually (so that the other side is left unworked for making the stitches in sts). Sometimes, you'll also need to make a stitch in the side of the stitch (in our example, stitches from round x, next to the chsp sts). The arrows show where to make the stitches:

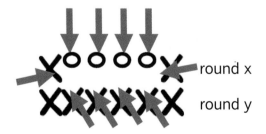

round x

round y

So whenever the pattern calls for working in the side of the stitch, these will be the sts next to the chain space.

Dimetrodon

Materials:

Yarn
Cotton-ish by Vickie Howell for Bernat,
70g balls, each approx. 282yd/258m

- 1 skein in Jade Jersey

Hook
Size C (2.75mm)

Other
4.5mm safety eyes

TIP
The sail can be easily done in stripes with a contrasting color of your choice, as it's worked flat, from side to side.

Head, body and tail:

Starting at the head

Ch2

Rnd 1 6sc in 2nd ch from the hook (6sts)
Rnd 2 inc six times (12sts)
Rnd 3 (2sc, inc) four times (16sts)
Rnd 4 1sc, inc, (3sc, inc) three times, 2sc (20sts)
Rnd 5–Rnd 7 20sc (20sts)
Rnd 8 7sc, inc, 1sc, 3in1, 1sc, inc, 8sc (24sts)
Rnd 9 8sc, (inc, 1sc) four times, 8sc (28sts)
Rnd 10–Rnd 13 28sc (28sts)

Insert safety eyes between rounds 7 and 8. Start stuffing and continue adding more as you go.

Rnd 14 (5sc, dec) four times (24sts)
Rnd 15 2sc, dec, (4sc, dec) three times, 2sc (20sts)
Rnd 16 4sc, dec, (3sc, dec) twice, 4sc (17 sts)
Rnd 17 17sc (17 sts)
Rnd 18 (4sc, inc) three times, 2sc (20 sts)
Rnd 19 (inc, 3sc) five times (25 sts)
Rnd 20 (4sc, inc) five times (30 sts)
Rnd 21 2sc, inc, (4sc, inc) five times, 2sc (36 sts)
Rnd 22–Rnd 23 36sc (36 sts)
Rnd 24 11sc, 3in1, 17sc, 3in1, 6sc (40 sts)
Rnd 25–Rnd 40 40sc (40 sts)
Rnd 41 21sc, dec, 5sc, dec, 10sc (38 sts)
Rnd 42 38sc (38 sts)
Rnd 43 18sc, dec, 9sc, dec, 7sc (36 sts)
Rnd 44 36sc (36 sts)
Rnd 45 (10sc, dec) three times (33 sts)
Rnd 46 4sc, dec, (9sc, dec) twice, 5sc (30 sts)
Rnd 47 30sc (30 sts)
Rnd 48 15sc, dec, 4sc, dec, 5sc, dec (27 sts)
Rnd 49 15sc, (dec, 3sc) twice, dec (24 sts)
Rnd 50 (2sc, dec) six times (18 sts)
Rnd 51–Rnd 52 18sc (18 sts)
Rnd 53 (4sc, dec) three times (15 sts)
Rnd 54 15sc (15 sts)
Rnd 55 (3sc, dec) three times (12 sts)
Rnd 56 12sc (12 sts)
Rnd 57 (2sc, dec) three times (9 sts)
Rnd 58 9sc (9 sts)
Rnd 59 (1sc, dec) three times (6 sts)
Rnd 60 6sc (6 sts)
Rnd 61 dec three times (3 sts)

Fasten off leaving a piece of yarn for sewing. Sew the opening closed.

Sail:

Ch2

Row 1 3in1, ch1, turn (3 sts)
Row 2 in FLO: 1sc, 3in1, 1sc, ch1, turn (5 sts)
Row 3 2sc, 3in1, 2sc, ch1, turn (7 sts)

Row 4 in FLO: 2sc, inc, 3in1, inc, 2sc, ch1, turn (11 sts)

Row 5 4sc, inc, 3in1, inc, 4sc, ch1, turn (15 sts)

Row 6 in FLO: 7sc, 3in1, 7sc, ch1, turn (17 sts)

Row 7 7sc, inc, 3in1, inc, 7sc, ch1, turn (21 sts)

Row 8 in FLO: 10sc, 3in1, 10sc, ch1, turn (23 sts)

Row 9 10sc, inc, 3in1, inc, 10sc, ch1, turn (27 sts)

Row 10 in FLO: 13sc, 3in1, 13sc, ch1, turn (29 sts)

Row 11 14sc, 3in1, 14sc, ch1, turn (31 sts)

Row 12 in FLO: 31sc, ch1, turn (31 sts)

Row 13 31sc, ch1, turn (31 sts)

Row 14– Row 19 repeat rows 12–13

Row 20 in FLO: 14sc, sc3tog, 14sc, ch1, turn (29 sts)

Row 21 13sc, sc3tog, 13sc, ch1, turn (27 sts)

Row 22 in FLO: 10sc, dec, sc3tog, dec, 10sc, ch1, turn (23 sts)

Row 23 10sc, sc3tog, 10sc, ch1, turn (21 sts)

Row 24 in FLO: 7sc, dec, sc3tog, dec, 7sc, ch1, turn (17 sts)

Row 25 7sc, sc3tog, 7sc, ch1, turn (15 sts)

Row 26 in FLO: 4sc, dec, sc3tog, dec, 4sc, ch1, turn (11 sts)

Row 27 2sc, dec, sc3tog, dec, 2sc (7 sts)

Row 28 in FLO: 2sc, sc3tog, 2sc (5 sts)

Row 29 1sc, sc3tog, 1sc (3 sts)

The sail does not require stuffing. Fasten off, leaving a piece of yarn for sewing.

Leg (make 4):

Starting at the foot

Ch2

Rnd 1 6sc in the second ch from the hook (6 sts)

Rnd 2 inc six times (12 sts)

Rnd 3 3sc, in FLO: [1sc, 1dc, ch2, 1sl st] in each of the the next 3sc, 6sc (9sc + 3 claws)

Rnd 4 3sc, sk claw stitches, work 1sc in each of the back loops left while making the claws, 6sc (12 sts)

Rnd 5 – Rnd 6 12sc (12 sts)

Rnd 7 (1sc, dec) three times, 3sc (9 sts)

Stuff the foot and add more as you go.

Rnd 8 – Rnd 10 9sc (9 sts)

Rnd 11 (dec, 1sc) three times (6 sts)

Fasten off leaving a piece of yarn for sewing. Sew the opening closed.

Assembling:

Sew the sail on dinosaur's back, starting at round 20 (to approx. round 47).

Attach the legs on both sides of the body approx. between rounds 23 & 24 and 42 & 43. If you want the legs to be movable, make sure that the yarn end is pulled out on the side of the leg, 1–2 rounds below the opening. Next, insert the needle in the body and through to the other side. Be careful to go between the stitches rather than through them. Take the other limb and run the needle through it. Then, insert the needle into the body exactly in the same place where it came from. Repeat with the yarn end from the other leg.

Ankylosaurus

Materials:

Yarn
Cotton-ish by Vickie Howell for Bernat,
70g balls, each approx. 282yd/258m

• 1 skein in Lemon Twill

Hook
Size C (2.75mm)

Other
2 4.5mm safety eyes

TIP
You can make more
or fewer horns and
attach them in
different places to
make your dino
special and
unique.

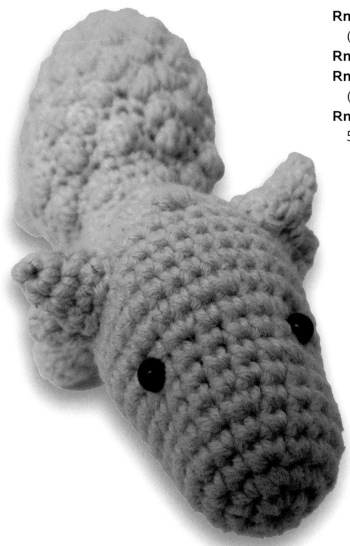

Rnd 10 13sc, (inc, 3sc) three times, 5sc (33 sts)

Rnd 11–Rnd 14 33sc (33 sts)

Rnd 15 10sc, bb, 9sc, bb, 9sc, bb, 2sc (33 sts)

Rnd 16 4sc, dec, (2sc, dec) three times, 5sc, (dec, 2sc) twice, 2sc (27 sts)

Insert safety eyes between rounds 8 & 9, about 8 sts apart. Start stuffing and continue adding more as you go.

Rnd 17 13sc, (dec, bb sts) twice, dec, 6sc (24 sts)

Rnd 18 (2sc, dec) twice, 1sc, bb, 1sc, dec, 2sc, bb, 2sc, dec, 1sc, bb, dec (19 sts)

Rnd 19 12sc, sk1, 6sc (18 sts)

Rnd 20 3sc, 3in1, 5sc, bb, 2sc, 3in1, 2sc, bb, 2sc (22 sts)

Rnd 21 3sc, inc, 1sc, inc, 16sc (24 sts)

Rnd 22 1sc, inc, 7sc, inc, 1sc, (bb, 3sc) three times, bb (26 sts)

Rnd 23 6sc, inc, 7sc, inc, (4sc, inc) twice, 1sc (30 sts)

Rnd 24 (4sc, inc) three times, (2sc, bb, 1sc, inc) three times (36 sts)

Rnd 25 4sc, ch3, sk3, 2sc, ch3, sk3, 11sc, bb, 5sc, bb, 6sc (30 + 2 chsp sts)

Rnd 26 4sc, 1sc in each ch, 2sc, 1sc in each ch, 8sc, (bb, 3sc) four times (36 sts)

Rnd 27 19sc, bb, 3sc, bb, 1sc, bb, 3in1, bb, 1sc, bb, 3sc, bb, 2sc (38 sts)

Rnd 28 21sc, bb, 1sc, inc, bb, 1sc, dec, bb, inc, bb, 1sc, inc, bb, 4sc (40 sts)

Rnd 29 3sc, inc, 9sc, inc, 5sc, (bb, 3sc) twice, bb, 3in1, (bb, 3sc) twice, bb, 2sc (44 sts)

Rnd 30 23sc, (bb, 3sc) five times, 1sc (44 sts)

Head, body and tail:
Starting at the head

Rnd 1 6sc in 2nd ch from the hook (6 sts)

Rnd 2 inc six times (12 sts)

Rnd 3 (1sc, inc) six times (18 sts)

Rnd 4 18sc (18 sts)

Rnd 5 (5sc, inc) x 3 (21 sts)

Rnd 6 21sc (21 sts)

Rnd 7 3sc, inc, (6sc, inc) twice, 3sc (24 sts)

Rnd 8 24sc (24 sts)

Rnd 9 7sc, (inc, 2sc) five times, inc, 1sc (30 sts)

Rnd 31 21sc, (bb, 3sc) five times, bb, 2sc (44 sts)

Rnd 32 Repeat round 30

Rnd 33 dec, 18sc, inc, (bb, 3sc) five times (42 sts)

Rnd 34 Repeat round 30

Rnd 35 Repeat round 31

Rnd 36 Repeat round 30

Rnd 37 Repeat round 31

Rnd 38 Repeat round 30

Rnd 39 Repeat round 32

Rnd 40 Repeat round 30

Rnd 41 Repeat round 31

Rnd 42 Repeat round 30

Rnd 43 Repeat round 32

Rnd 44 Repeat round 30

Rnd 45 5sc, ch3, sk3, 4sc, ch3, sk3, 5sc, dec, (bb, 3sc) five times, dec (36 sc + 2 ch3 sp sts)

Rnd 46 2sc, dec, 1sc, 1sc in each ch, 4sc, 1sc in each ch, 3sc, dec, 4sc, (bb, 3sc) four times, bb, 1sc (40 sts)

Rnd 47 19sc, dec (bb, 3sc) four times, bb, dec, (38 sts)

Rnd 48 (4sc, dec) three times, 3sc, (bb, 1sc, dec) three times, bb, dec (30 sts)

Rnd 49 (2sc, dec) four times, (2sc, bb sts) four times, 2sc (26 sts)

Rnd 50 (dec, 1sc) five times, (bb, 2sc) three times, dec (20 sts)

11

Rnd 51 1sc, dec, 3sc, dec, 12sc (18 sts)
Rnd 52 10sc, bb, 2sc, bb, 4sc (18 sts)
Rnd 53 18sc (18 sts)
Rnd 54 1sc, dec, 4sc, dec, 3sc, bb, dec, 3sc (15 sts)
Rnd 55–Rnd 57 15sc (15 sts)
Rnd 58 (3sc, dec) three times (12 sts)
Rnd 59 12sc (12 sts)
Rnd 60. (2sc, dec) three times (9 sts)
Rnd 61 9sc (9 sts)
Rnd 62 1sc, 3in1, 3sc, 3in1, 3sc (13 sts)
Rnd 63 2sc, 3in1, 5sc, 3in1, 4sc (17 sts)
Rnd 64 17sc (17 sts)
Rnd 68 2sc, sc3tog, 2sc, dec, 2sc, sc3tog, 3sc (12 sts)
Rnd 69 (1sc, dec) four times (8 sts)
Rnd 70 dec four times (4 sts)

Fasten off, sew the opening closed.

Horns

You can stuff the horns lightly.

Bigger horn (make 2):

Ch2
Rnd 1 4sc in 2nd ch from the hook (4 sts)
Rnd 2 (inc, 1sc) twice (6 sts)
Rnd 3 (1sc, inc) three times (9 sts)
Rnd 4 inc twice, 7sc (11 sts)

Fasten off, leaving a piece of yarn for sewing.

Smaller horn (make 2):

Ch2
Rnd 1 4sc in 2nd ch from the hook (4 sts)
Rnd 2 (inc, 1sc) twice (6 sts)
Rnd 3 (1sc, inc) three times (9 sts)

Fasten off, leaving a piece of yarn for sewing.

Legs:

We will now work in each chsp hole to make legs.

Join yarn to the first sc skipped in round 25, ch 1.

Rnd 1 1sc in each sc (3), inc in the side of sc (2), 1sc in each ch (3), inc in the side of sc (2) (10 sts)

Rnd 2–Rnd 4 10sc (10 sts)

Rnd 5 inc three times, 3sc, inc, 3sc (14 sts)

Rnd 6 (inc, 1sc) four times, 6sc (18 sts)

Rnd 7 18sc (18 sts)

Rnd 8 (1sc, dec) six times (12 sts)

Stuff the leg.

Rnd 9 dec six times (6sts)

Fasten off, sew the opening closed. Repeat for every hole (rounds 25 and 45).

Assembling:

Sew the horns symmetrically on both sides of the head, approx. between rounds 13 & 15.

Materials:

Yarn
Cotton-ish by Vickie Howell for Bernat,
70g balls, each approx. 282yd/258m

- 1 skein in Lemon Twill
- 1 skein in Cotton Harvest

Hook
Size C (2.75mm)

Other
6mm safety eyes

TIP
You can try joining
rounds 1–8 with a
sl so that the spikes
are distributed
more evenly.

Head:

Starting at the top

Ch2

Rnd 1 6sc in 2nd ch from the hook (6sts)
Rnd 2 inc six times (12sts)
Rnd 3 (1sc, inc) six times (18sts)
Rnd 4 (2sc, inc) six times (24sts)
Rnd 5 1sc, (inc, 3sc) five times, inc, 2sc (30sts)
Rnd 6–Rnd 7 30sc (30sts)
Rnd 8 1sc, *change to CC, [1sc, ch2, 1sl in the 2nd ch, 1sc where the last sc was made] in the next st, change to MC, 2sc*, rep from * to * 8 times, change to CC, [1sc, ch2, 1sl in the 2nd ch, 1sc where the last sc was made], 1sc (30sc plus spikes)
Rnd 9 2sc, (sk spike, 3sc) four times, sk spike, inc, 3in1, inc, (sk spike, 3sc) four times, sk spike, 1sc (34sts)
Rnd 10 15sc, inc, 1sc, 3in1, 1sc, inc, 14sc (38sts)
Rnd 11 3sc, *change to CC [1sc, ch3, 1sc in 2nd and 3rd ch, 1 sc where the last sc was made], in the next st, change to MC*, 2sc, repeat once more, 8sc, inc, *change to CC [1sc, ch1, 1sl where the last sc was made], in the next st, change to MC*, 2sc, 3in1, 2sc, change to CC [1sc, ch1, 1sl where the last sc was made], in the next st, change to MC, inc, 8sc, *change to CC [1sc, ch3, 1 sc in the 2nd and 3rd ch, 1sc where the lawas made], in the next st, change to MC, 2 sc*, repeat once more (41sc plus horns).
Rnd 12 4sc, sk spike, 3sc, sk spike, 10sc, sk spike, 2sc, inc, 1sc, inc, 2sc, sk spike, 11sc, sk spike, 3sc, sk spike, 2sc (42sts)
Rnd 13 – Rnd 16 42sc (42sts)

Insert safety eyes between rounds 11 & 12, on both sides of the muzzle. Start stuffing and continue adding more as you go.

Rnd 17 15sc, dec, 4sc, dec twice, 4sc, dec, 11sc (38sts)

Rnd 18 12sc, dec, 4sc, dec, 2sc, dec, 4sc, dec, 8sc (34sts)
Rnd 19 1sc, dec, 11sc, (dec, 2sc) three times, 8sc (30sts)
Rnd 20 (3sc, dec) six times (24sts)
Rnd 21 8sc, (sc3tog, 1sc) three times, 4sc (18sts)
Rnd 22–Rnd 23 18sc (18sts)

Rnd 24 10sc, inc, 7sc (19sts)
Rnd 25 9sc, inc, 2sc, inc, 6sc (21sts)
Rnd 26 (6sc, inc) three times (24sts)
Rnd 27–Rnd 28 24sc (24sts)
Rnd 29 9sc, ch3, sk3, 5sc, ch3, sk3, 4sc
  (18 + 2 ch-3sps)
Rnd 30 9sc, 1sc in each ch, 2sc, inc, 2sc,
  1sc in each ch, 4sc (25sts)
Rnd 31 (4sc, inc) five times (30sts)

You may want to move to making the arms
now, as it'll be easier to stuff them and
secure the ends at this point. This can,
however, be done at the very end as well.

Rnd 32 30sc (30sts)
Rnd 33 2sc, inc, (5sc, inc) four times, 3sc
  (35sts)
Rnd 24–Rnd 35 35sc (35sts)
Rnd 36 (6sc, inc) five times (40sts)
Rnd 37 40sc (40sts)
Rnd 38 5sc, 3in1, 34sc (42sts)
Rnd 39 6sc, 3in1, 16sc, dec, 5sc, dec, 10sc
  (42sts)
Rnd 40 4sc, inc, 5sc, inc, 10sc, dec, 11sc,
  dec, 6sc (42sts)
Rnd 41–Rnd 42 42sc (42sts)
Rnd 43 4sc, dec, ch5, sk5, dec, (5sc, dec)
  four times, 1sc (36 plus ch5sp)
Rnd 44 5sc, 1sc in each ch, 8sc, (dec, 4sc)
  three times (33sts)
Rnd 45 15sc, (dec, 3sc) three times, 3sc
  (30sts)
Rnd 46 3sc, dec, (2sc, dec) twice, 4sc, dec,
  (3sc, dec) twice, 1sc (24sts)

You may want to move to making the tail
now, as it'll be easier to stuff it and secure
the ends at this point. This can, however, be
done after the body is finished.

Rnd 47 (dec, 2sc) six times (18sts)
Rnd 48 (1sc, dec) six times (12sts)
Rnd 49 dec six times (6sts)

Fasten off, sew the opening closed.

Arms

If you're making the arms after finishing
round 31, stuff them when you're done
sewing the opening closed. If you make
them at the end, stuff them at round 6 and
add a bit more stuffing later, if needed.

Right arm:

Join yarn to the first sc skipped in round 29,
ch1 (in the first hole – to make the right arm).

Rnd 1 1sc in each sc (3), 1sc in the side of
  sc (1), 1sc in each ch (3), 1sc in the side
  of sc (1) (8sts)
Rnd 2–Rnd 4 8sc (8sts)
Rnd 5 dec, 2sc, 3in1, 1sc, dec (8sts)

Rnd 6 (inc, 3sc) twice (10sts)
Rnd 7 10sc (10sts)
Rnd 8 dec five times (5sts)

Fasten off, sew the opening closed.

Left arm:

Join yarn to the first sc skipped in round 29, ch1 (in the second hole–to make the left arm sts).

Rnd 1 1sc in each sc (3), 1sc in the side of sc (1), 1sc in each ch (3), 1sc in the side of sc (1) (8sts)
Rnd 2–Rnd 4 8sc (8sts)
Rnd 5 3in1, 1sc, dec twice, 2sc (8sts)
Rnd 6 1sc, inc, 3sc, inc, 2sc (10sts)
Rnd 7 10sc (10sts)
Rnd 8 dec five times (5sts)

Fasten off, sew the opening closed.

Tail:

If you're making the tail after finishing round 46, stuff it when you're done sewing the opening closed. If you make it at the end, stuff it at round 8, adding a bit more stuffing as you go.

Join yarn to the first sc skipped in round 43, ch 1.

Rnd 1 1sc in each of the first 2sc, inc in next sc, 1sc in each of the next 2sc (6), 1sc in the side of sc (1), 1sc in each of the first 2ch, inc in next ch, 1sc in each of the next 2ch (6), 1sc in the side of sc (1) (14sts)
Rnd 2–Rnd 6 14sc (14sts)
Rnd 7 (dec, 5sc) twice (12sts)
Rnd 8 12sc (12sts)
Rnd 9 (2sc, dec) three times (9sts)
Rnd 10 9sc (9sts)
Rnd 11 (1sc, dec) three times (6sts)

Fasten off, sew the opening closed.

Leg (make 2):

Starting at the foot

Ch5
Rnd 1 1sc in 2nd ch from the hook, 2sc, 4in1, 2sc, inc (11sts)
Rnd 2 inc, 2sc, inc four times, 2sc, inc twice (18sts)
Rnd 3 inc, 3sc, (inc, 1sc) four times, 2sc, (inc, 1sc) twice (25sts)
Rnd 4–Rnd 6 25sc (25sts)
Rnd 7 4sc, (dec, 1sc) five times, 6sc (20sts)
Rnd 8 dec, 3sc, sc3tog three times, 3sc, dec, 1sc (12sts)
Rnd 9–Rnd 13 12sc (12sts)

Stuff the leg and continue adding more as you go.

Rnd 14 6sc, 3in1, 5sc (14sts)
Rnd 15 (inc, 6sc) twice (16sts)
Rnd 16–Rnd 18 16sc (16sts)
Rnd 19 (dec, 2sc) four times (12sts)
Rnd 20 dec six times (6sts)

Fasten off, leaving a piece of yarn for sewing.

Assembling:

Attach the legs on both sides of the body approx. between rounds 44 & 45. If you want the legs to be movable, make sure that the yarn end is pulled out on the side of the leg, 1–2 rounds below the opening. Next, insert the needle in the body and through to the other side. Be careful to go between the stitches rather than through them. Take the other limb and run the needle through it. Then, insert the needle into the body exactly in the same place where it came from.

Repeat with the yarn end from the other leg.

Stegosaurus

Materials:

Yarn
Cotton-ish by Vickie Howell for Bernat, 70g balls, each approx. 282yd/258m

- 1 skein in Seersucker

Hook
Size C (2.75mm)

Other
4.5mm safety eyes

TIP
You can try adding more or fewer spikes in different sizes and colors.

Head, body and tail:
Starting at the head

Ch2

Rnd 1 6sc in the 2nd ch from the hook (6 sts)

Rnd 2 (inc, 1sc) three times (9 sts)

Rnd 3 (2sc, inc) three times (12 sts)

Rnd 4 12sc (12 sts)

Rnd 5 (3sc, inc) three times (15 sts)

Rnd 6–Rnd 7 15sc (15 sts)

Rnd 8 4sc, inc twice, 3sc, inc twice, 4sc (19 sts)

Rnd 9 19sc (19 sts)

Rnd 10 5sc, dec twice, 1sc, dec twice, 5sc (15 sts)

Insert safety eyes between rounds 7 & 8 (under the first and last "inc" from round 8 sts). Start stuffing and continue adding more as you go.

Rnd 11–Rnd 14 15sc (15 sts)

Rnd 15 7sc, inc, 3sc in 1, inc, 5sc (19 sts)

Rnd 16 19sc (19 sts)

Rnd 17 inc twice, 7sc, inc, 3sc in 1, inc, 7sc (25 sts)

Rnd 18 25sc (25 sts)

Rnd 19 1sc, inc, 2sc, inc, 8sc, inc, 3in1, inc, 9sc (31 sts)

Rnd 20 31sc (31 sts)

Rnd 21 inc, 4sc, inc, 12sc, inc, 3sc in 1, inc, 10sc (37 sts)

Rnd 22 37sc (37 sts)

Rnd 23 4sc, inc, (7sc, inc) twice, 5sc, inc, 7sc, inc, 2sc (42 sts)

Rnd 24–Rnd 27 42sc (42 sts)

Rnd 28 25sc, inc twice, 15sc (44 sts)

Rnd 29–Rnd 32 44sc (44 sts)

Rnd 33 24sc, dec, 3sc, dec, 13sc (42 sts)

Rnd 24–Rnd 37 42sc (42 sts)

Rnd 38 12sc, (dec, 3sc) six times (36 sts)

Rnd 39 36sc (36 sts)

Rnd 40 dec, 8sc, dec, (3sc, dec) twice, 4sc, (dec, 3sc) twice (30 sts)

Rnd 41 30sc (30 sts)

Rnd 42 (3sc, dec) six times (24 sts)

Rnd 43 24sc (24 sts)

Rnd 44 (dec, 2sc) six times (18 sts)

Rnd 45 18sc (18 sts)

Rnd 46 (4sc, dec) three times (15 sts)

Rnd 47–Rnd 48 15sc (15 sts)

Rnd 49 (3sc, dec) three times (12 sts)

Rnd 50–Rnd 51 12sc (12 sts)

Rnd 52 (2sc, dec) three times (9 sts)

Rnd 53 6sc, in FLO:[1sl st, ch4, 1 sl in the 2nd, 3rd and 4th ch from the hook], 1sc, in FLO:[1sl st, ch4, 1 sl in the 2nd, 3rd and 4th ch from the hook] (9 sts)

Rnd 54 6sc, 1sc in sl st, sk spike, 1sc, 1sc in sl st, sk spike (9 sts)

Rnd 55 6sc, in FLO:[1sl st, ch3, 1 sl in the 2nd and 3rd ch from the hook], 1sc, in FLO:[1sl st, ch3, 1 sl in the 2nd and 3rd ch from the hook] (9 sts)

Rnd 56 6sc, 1sc in sl st, sk spike, 1sc, 1sc in sl st, sk spike (9 sts)

Rnd 57 (1sc, sc2tog sts) three times (6 sts)

Rnd 58 dec, sk the rest (1 st)

Fasten off, sew the opening closed.

Spikes

Small (make 4):

Ch2

Rnd 1 4sc in the 2nd ch from the hook (4 sts)
Rnd 2 (inc, 1sc) twice (6 sts)
Rnd 3 (3in1, 2sc) twice (10 sts)
Rnd 4 10sc (10 sts)
Rnd 5 dec five times (5 sts)

Fasten off, leaving a long piece of yarn for sewing.

Medium (make 4):

Ch2

Rnd 1 4sc in the 2nd ch from the hook (4 sts)
Rnd 2 (inc, 1sc) twice (6 sts)
Rnd 3 (inc, 2sc) twice (8 sts)
Rnd 4 (3 in1, 3sc) twice (12 sts)
Rnd 5 12sc (12 sts)
Rnd 6 (sc3tog, dec, 1sc) twice (6 sts)

Fasten off, leaving a long piece of yarn for sewing.

Big (make 4):

Ch2

Rnd 1 6sc in the 2nd ch from the hook (6 sts)
Rnd 2 (inc, 2sc) twice (8 sts)
Rnd 3 (3in1, 3sc) twice (12 sts)
Rnd 4 12sc (12 sts)
Rnd 5 1sc, inc, 5sc, inc, 4sc (14 sts)
Rnd 6 14sc (14 sts)

Rnd 7 dec, sc3tog, dec twice, sc3tog, dec
   (6 sts)

Fasten off, leaving a long piece of yarn for
sewing.

Large (make 2):

Ch2

Rnd 1 6sc in the 2nd ch from the hook (6 sts)
Rnd 2 (inc, 2sc) twice (8 sts)
Rnd 3 (inc, 3sc) twice (10 sts)
Rnd 4 (3in1, 4sc) twice (14 sts)
Rnd 5 1sc, inc, 6sc, inc, 5sc (16 sts)
Rnd 6–7 16sc (16 sts)
Rnd 8 (sc3tog, 5sc) twice (12 sts)
Rnd 9 dec six times (6 sts)

Fasten off, leaving a long piece of yarn for
sewing.

Front leg (make 2):
Starting at the foot

Ch2

Rnd 1 6sc in the 2nd ch from the hook
   (6 sts)
Rnd 2 inc twice, 3in1 twice, inc twice (14 sts)
Rnd 3 in BLO: 14sc (14 sts)
Rnd 4 14sc (14 sts)
Rnd 5 4sc, dec three times, 4sc (11 sts)
Rnd 6–**Rnd 8** 11sc (11 sts)

Stuff the foot and continue stuffing as you
go, remembering to stuff the upper part very
lightly.

Rnd 9 5sc, inc, 5sc (12 sts)
Rnd 10 (2sc, inc) four times (16 sts)
Rnd 11–**Rnd 12** 16sc (16 sts)
Rnd 13 dec eight times (8 sts)

Fasten off, leaving a long piece of yarn for
sewing. Sew the opening closed by pulling the
yarn end through the front loops of all stitches
from the laround. Then, pull the yarn below the
9th round, to the side (to the left in one leg and
to the right in the second one sts).

Back leg (make 2):

Starting at the foot

Ch2

Rnd 1 6sc in the 2nd ch from the hook (6 sts)
Rnd 2 inc, 3in1 three times, inc twice (15 sts)
Rnd 3 in BLO: 15sc (15 sts)
Rnd 4 15sc (15 sts)
Rnd 5 4sc, dec three times, 5sc (12 sts)

Stuff the foot and continue stuffing as you go, remembering to stuff the upper part very lightly.

Rnd 6–Rnd 9 12sc (12 sts)
Rnd 10 (inc, 2sc) four times (16 sts)
Rnd 11 7sc, inc, 2sc, inc, 5sc (18 sts)
Rnd 12 18sc (18 sts)
Rnd 13 (2sc, dec) four times, 2sc (14 sts)
Rnd 14 dec seven times (7 sts)

Fasten off, leaving a long piece of yarn for sewing. Sew the opening closed.

Assembling:

Attach the legs on both sides of the body, front between rounds 22 & 23, back between rounds 37 & 38. If you want the legs to be movable, make sure that the yarn end is pulled out on the side of the leg, 1–2 rounds below the opening. Next, insert the needle in the body and through to the other side. Be careful to go between the stitches rather than through them. Take the other limb and run the needle through it. Then, insert the needle into the body exactly in the same place where it came from. Repeat with the yarn end from the other leg.

Sew the spikes on the dino's back: starting at round 15 attach a small spike, then medium, big, large, big, medium, small in two rows.

Mosasaurus

Materials:

Yarn
Cotton-ish by Vickie Howell for Bernat, 70g balls, each approx. 282yd/258m

- 1 skein in Spinning Jenny

Hook
Size C (2.75mm)

Other
4.5mm safety eyes

TIP
You can embroider some stripes or dots with a contrasting color on his back to customize him a bit.

Head, body and tail:
Starting at the nose

Ch2

Rnd 1 6sc in 2nd ch from the hook (6 sts)

Rnd 2 (1sc, inc) three times (9 sts)

Rnd 3 (2sc, inc) three times (12 sts)

Rnd 4 12sc (12 sts)

Rnd 5 (3sc, inc) three times (15 sts)

Rnd 6 15sc (15 sts)

Rnd 7 (4sc, inc) three times (18 sts)

Rnd 8–**Rnd 9** 18sc (18 sts)

Rnd 10 (5sc, inc) three times (21 sts)

Rnd 11–**Rnd 12** 21sc (21 sts)

Rnd 13 2sc, (inc, 1sc) four times, inc, 10sc (26 sts)

Rnd 14 (3sc, inc) four times, 10sc (30 sts)

Rnd 15–**Rnd 20** 30sc (30 sts)

Insert safety eyes between rounds 13 & 14, about 9 stitches apart. Start stuffing and continue adding more as you go.

Rnd 21 7sc, (dec, 2sc) twice, dec, 7sc, inc, 4sc, inc (29 sts)

Rnd 22 25sc, inc, 3sc (30 sts)

Rnd 23 inc, 19sc, inc, 9sc (32 sts)

Rnd 24 (7sc, inc) four times (36 sts)

Rnd 25 36sc (36 sts)

Rnd 26 3sc, (inc, 9sc) twice, inc, 12sc (39 sts)

Rnd 27 39sc (39 sts)

Rnd 28 9sc, inc, 10sc, inc, 13sc, inc, 4sc (42 sts)

Rnd 29–Rnd 44 42sc (42 sts)

Rnd 45 (12sc, dec) three times (39 sts)

Rnd 46 5sc, (dec, 11sc) twice, dec, 6sc (36 sts)

Rnd 47 (10sc, dec) three times (33 sts)

Rnd 48 33sc (33 sts)

Rnd 49 4sc, (dec, 9sc) twice, dec, 5sc (30 sts)

Rnd 50 30sc (30 sts)

Rnd 51 4sc, (dec, 8sc) twice, dec, 4sc (27 sts)

Rnd 52 27sc (27 sts)

Rnd 53 7sc, (dec, 3sc) twice, dec, 8sc (24 sts)

Rnd 54 24sc (24 sts)

Rnd 55 6sc, (dec, 3sc) twice, dec, 6sc (21 sts)

Rnd 56 21sc (21 sts)

Rnd 57 (5sc, dec) three times (18 sts)

Rnd 58–Rnd 59 18sc (18 sts)

Rnd 60 (4sc, dec) three times (15 sts)

Rnd 61–Rnd 62 15sc (15 sts)

Rnd 63 (3sc, dec) three times (12 sts)

Rnd 64–Rnd 65 12sc (12 sts)

The rest of the tail does not require stuffing.

Rnd 66 7sc, 3in1 twice, 3sc (16 sts)

Rnd 67–Rnd 71 (16 sts)

Rnd 72 2sc, dec, 12sc (15 sts)

Rnd 73 (3sc, dec) three times (12 sts)

Rnd 74 1sc, dec, (2sc, dec) twice, 1sc (9 sts)

Rnd 75 (dec, 1sc) three times (6 sts)

Fasten off, leaving a piece of yarn for sewing. Sew the opening closed.

Flipper (make 4):

Ch2

Rnd 1 6sc in 2nd ch from the hook (6 sts)
Rnd 2 inc six times (12 sts)
Rnd 3 (inc, 5sc) twice (14 sts)
Rnd 4 14sc (14 sts)
Rnd 5 (inc, 6sc) twice (16 sts)
Rnd 6 16sc (16 sts)
Rnd 7 2sc, dec, 4sc, inc twice, 4sc, dec (16 sts)

Rnd 8 dec, 14sc (15 sts)
Rnd 9–Rnd 11 1sc, dec, 4sc, inc twice, 4sc, dec (15 sts)
Rnd 12 dec, 11sc, dec (13 sts).

Fasten off, leaving a long piece of yarn for sewing. Flippers don't require stuffing.

Assembling:

Sew the front flippers between rounds 25 & 31 and back ones between rounds 48 & 54.

Corythosaurus

Materials:

Yarn
Cotton-ish by Vickie Howell for Bernat,
70g balls, each approx. 282yd/258m

- 1 skein in Crimson Twine

Hook
Size C (2.75mm)

Other
6mm safety eyes

TIP
If you'd like to have a clearer border between the head and the crest, you can try working the first 8-9 rounds in BLO, or in a different color. It would be a good idea to work them as joined rounds rather than in spirals, too.

Head and body:
Starting at the top of the head

Ch2

Rnd 1 6sc in 2nd ch from the hook (6 sts)
Rnd 2 inc twice (12 sts)
Rnd 3 (1sc, inc) six times (18 sts)
Rnd 4 (inc, 8sc) twice (20 sts)
Rnd 5 20sc (20 sts)
Rnd 6 (inc, 9sc) twice (22 sts)
Rnd 7 22sc (22 sts)
Rnd 8 (10sc, inc) twice (24 sts)
Rnd 9 11sc, 3in1, 11sc, inc (27 sts)
Rnd 10 12sc, 3in1, 14sc (29 sts)
Rnd 11 14sc, ch6, 1sc in 2nd ch from the hook and in next 4ch, 1sc in the next sc of the previous round (where the last sc before ch4 was made), 15sc (35 + 5 loops on the other side of the ch6)
Rnd 12 14sc, 1 sc in the next 4 loops on the other side of the ch from the previous round, 3in1 in the last loop, inc, 14sc, (inc, 1sc) three times (46 sts)
Rnd 13 (inc, 1sc) twice, 9sc, inc, 2sc, inc, 3sc, 3in1, 3sc, inc, 1sc, inc, 12sc, (inc, 2sc) twice, inc (57 sts)
Rnd 14 25sc, 3in1, 31sc (59 sts)
Rnd 15–Rnd 16 59sc (59 sts)
Rnd 17 18sc, (dec, 2sc) five times, 21sc (54 sts)
Rnd 18 16sc (dec, 1sc) six times, 20sc (48 sts)
Rnd 19 2sc, dec, 12sc, dec twice, sc3tog, dec twice, 13sc, dec, 3sc, dec, 1sc (39 sts)
Rnd 20 dec, 10sc, dec twice, sc3tog, dec twice, 10sc, (dec, 1sc) twice (30 sts)
Rnd 21 dec, 7sc, dec four times, 7sc, (dec, 1sc) twice (23 sts)
Rnd 22 4sc, dec, 9sc, dec, 6sc (21 sts)

Insert safety eyes between rounds 13 and 14. Stuff the head (don't add too much stuffing to the crest) and continue adding more as you go.

Rnd 23 1sc, (dec, 5sc) twice, dec, 4sc (18 sts)
Rnd 24 18sc (18 sts)
Rnd 25 5sc, dec, 2sc, dec, 5sc, inc twice (18 sts)
Rnd 26 18sc (18 sts)
Rnd 27 inc, 3sc, dec, 3sc, dec, 4sc, inc, 2sc (18 sts)
Rnd 28–Rnd 30 18sc (18 sts)
Rnd 31 17sc, 3in1 (20 sts)
Rnd 32 (4sc, inc) three times, 3sc, 3in1, 1sc (25 sts)
Rnd 33 22sc, 3in1, 2sc (27 sts)
Rnd 34 (5sc, inc) three times, 5sc, 3in1, 3sc (32 sts)
Rnd 35 27sc, 3in1, 4sc (34 sts)
Rnd 36 28sc, 3in1, 5sc (36 sts)
Rnd 37 (inc, 5sc) six times (42 sts)
Rnd 38 (6sc, inc) six times (48 sts)
Rnd 39–Rnd 40 48sc (48 sts)
Rnd 41 16sc, dec, 22sc, inc, 7sc (48 sts)
Rnd 42 12sc, dec, 5sc, dec, 18sc, inc twice, 7sc (48 sts)
Rnd 43–Rnd 44 48sc (48 sts)
Rnd 45 (9sc, dec) twice, 17sc, 3in1, 8sc (48 sts)
Rnd 46 11sc, dec, 3sc, dec, 18sc, inc, 3sc, inc, 7sc (48 sts)
Rnd 47–Rnd 48 48sc (48 sts)
Rnd 49 (9sc, dec) twice, 16sc, 3in1, 9sc (48 sts)
Rnd 50 11sc, dec, 3sc, 19sc, 3in1, 10sc (48 sts)
Rnd 51–Rnd 52 48sc (48 sts)
Rnd 53 7sc, dec, 9sc, dec, 14sc, inc, 5sc, inc, 7sc (48 sts)
Rnd 54 (5sc, dec) three times, 12sc, (inc, 2sc) three times, 6sc (48 sts)
Rnd 55 (dec, 5sc) four times, 6sc, 3in1, 13sc (46 sts)
Rnd 56 (4sc, dec) three times, 26sc, dec (42 sts)
Rnd 57 (3sc, dec) four times, 6 sc, ch8, sk6, (3sc, dec) twice (30sc +ch8sp)

Rnd 58 1sc, (dec, 4sc) three times, dec twice, 5sc, dec twice, 4sc, dec (30 sts)
Rnd 59 (3sc, dec) six times (24 sts)
Rnd 60 1sc, (dec, 2sc) five times, dec, 1sc (18 sts)
Rnd 61 (dec, 1sc) six times (12 sts)
Rnd 62 dec six times (6 sts)

Fasten off, leaving a piece of yarn for sewing. Sew the opening closed.

Tail:

Join yarn to the first sc skipped in round 34, ch 1.

Rnd 1 1sc in each of the skipped sc (6), 1sc to the side of sc (1), 1sc in each ch (8), 1sc to the side of sc (16 sts)
Rnd 2 16sc (16 sts)
Rnd 3 (6, dec) twice (14 sts)
Rnd 4 14sc (14 sts)
Start stuffing and continue adding more as you go.
Rnd 5 2sc, dec, 5sc, dec, 3sc (12 sts)
Rnd 6 (dec, 2sc) three times (9 sts)
Rnd 7 9sc (9 sts)
Rnd 8 (dec, 1sc) three times (6 sts)
Rnd 9 6sc (6 sts)
Rnd 10 dec, 1sc, dec, leave the last unworked

Fasten off, sew the opening closed.

Arm (make 2):
Starting at the "hand"

Ch2

Rnd 1 6sc in 2nd ch from the hook (6 sts)
Rnd 2 1sc, 3in1, 2sc, 3in1, 1sc (10 sts)
Rnd 3 (inc, 1sc) five times (15 sts)
Rnd 4–Rnd 6 15sc (15 sts)
Stuff the leg and continue adding more as you go.
Rnd 7 dec, 11sc, dec (13 sts)
Rnd 8–Rnd 20 13sc (13 sts)
Rnd 21 1sc, dec, 10sc (12 sts)

Rnd 22 dec six times (6 sts)

Fasten off, leaving a piece of yarn for sewing.

Leg (make 2):

Starting at the top

Ch2
Rnd 1 6sc in 2nd ch from the hook (6 sts)
Rnd 2 inc six times (12 sts)
Rnd 3 (1sc, inc) six times (18 sts)
Rnd 4 (inc, 8sc) twice (20 sts)
Rnd 5–Rnd 8 20sc (20 sts)
Rnd 9 (dec, 8sc) twice (18 sts)
Rnd 10 18sc (18 sts)
Rnd 11 (dec, 2sc) three times, 6sc (15 sts)
Rnd 12–Rnd 14 15sc (15 sts)
Rnd 15 3in1, 6sc, dec, 6sc (16 sts)
Rnd 16 1sc, 3in1, 14sc (18 sts)
Rnd 17 2sc, 3in1, 15sc (20 sts)
Rnd 18 2sc, inc, 1sc, 3in1, 1sc, inc, 13sc (24 sts)
Rnd 19 3sc, inc twice, 1sc, 3in1, 1sc, inc twice, 14sc (30 sts)
Rnd 20–Rnd 21 30sc (30 sts)
Rnd 22 3sc, (dec, 2sc) three times, 3sc, (dec, 2sc) three times (24 sts)

Rnd 23 (1sc, dec) eight times (16 sts)
Rnd 24 (1sc, dec, sc3tog, dec) twice (8 sts)

Fasten off, leaving a long piece of yarn for sewing. Sew the opening closed. Pull the yarn end to the upper part of the leg (between rounds 4 and 5 sts) to sew it to the body—it'll flatten the sole at the same time.

Assembling:

Sew the arms and legs on both sides of the dinosaur's body, approx. between rounds 31 & 32 and rounds 48 & 49. If you want the joints to be movable, make sure that the yarn end is pulled out on the side of the limb, in its upper part. Next, insert the needle in the body and through to the other side. Be careful to go between the stitches rather than through them. Take the other limb and run the needle through it. Then, insert the needle into the body exactly in the same place where it came from. Repeat with the yarn end from the other limb.

Apatosaurus

Materials:

Yarn
Cotton-ish by Vickie Howell for Bernat,
70g balls, each approx. 282yd/258m

- 1 skein in Cotton Field

Hook
Size C (2.75mm)

Other
6mm safety eyes

TIP
If you'd rather have the legs stationary and sewn under the belly instead of on the sides, you can fasten off after round 16, stuff and attach them.

Head:

Starting at the nose

Ch2

Rnd 1 6sc in 2nd ch from the hook (6 sts)
Rnd 2 inc six times (12 sts)
Rnd 3 (3sc, inc) three times (15 sts)
Rnd 4 15sc (15 sts)
Rnd 5 1sc, inc, (4sc, inc) twice, 3sc (18 sts)
Rnd 6 18sc (18 sts)
Rnd 7 (5sc, inc) three times (21 sts)
Rnd 8 2sc, inc, (6sc, inc) twice, 4sc (24 sts)
Rnd 9–Rnd 10 24sc (24 sts)
Rnd 11 6sc, (inc, 3sc) three times, 6sc (27 sts)
Rnd 12 9sc, inc, (4sc, inc) twice, 7sc (30 sts)
Rnd 13 (inc, 9sc) three times (33 sts)
Rnd 14 6sc, inc, (10sc, inc) twice, 4sc (36 sts)
Rnd 15 1sc, dec, 15sc, inc, 2sc, inc, 12sc, dec (36 sts)
Rnd 16 36sc (36 sts)
Rnd 17 (5sc, inc) six times (42 sts)

Insert safety eyes between rounds 11 & 12. Start stuffing and continue adding more as you go.

Rnd 18–Rnd 19 42sc (42 sts)
Rnd 20 (5sc, dec) twice, 5sc, ch7, sk9, (5sc, dec) twice (29 + ch7sp sts)
Rnd 21 2sc, dec, 4sc, dec, 5sc, dec, 1sc in next 7ch, dec, 5sc, dec, 3sc (31 sts)
Rnd 22 (3sc, dec) twice, 2sc, dec, 2sc, sc3tog, 2sc, (dec, 3sc) twice (24 sts)
Rnd 23 (dec, 2sc) six times (18 sts)
Rnd 24 (1sc, dec) six times (12 sts)
Rnd 25 dec six times (6 sts)

Fasten off, leaving a piece of yarn for sewing.

Crest:

Join yarn to the first sc skipped in round 20, ch 1.

Rnd 1 Make 1sc in each of the skipped sts (9), inc in the side of sc (2), 1sc in each ch (7), inc in the side of sc (2) (20 sts)
Rnd 2–Rnd 3 20sc (20 sts)
Rnd 4 (4sc, dec) twice, 3sc, inc, 2sc, dec (18 sts)
Rnd 5 2sc, dec, 1sc, dec, 5sc, (inc, 2sc) twice (18 sts)
Rnd 6 (7sc, dec) twice (16 sts)
Rnd 7 16sc (16 sts)
Rnd 8 3sc, dec, 11sc (15 sts)
Rnd 9 (dec, 3sc) three times (12 sts)
Rnd 10 12sc (12 sts)

Start stuffing and continue adding more as you go.

Rnd 11 2sc, dec, 4sc, inc, 3sc (12 sts)
Rnd 12 1sc, sc3tog, 3sc, inc twice, 3sc (12 sts)
Rnd 13 dec three times, 6sc (9 sts)
Rnd 14 3sc, sc3tog twice (5 sts)

Fasten off, sew the opening closed.

Tail and body:
Starting at the tail

Ch2

Rnd 1 6sc in 2nd ch from the hook (6 sts)
Rnd 2 (1sc, inc) three times (9 sts)
Rnd 3 9sc (9 sts)
Rnd 4 (inc, 2sc) three times (12 sts)
Rnd 5–Rnd 6 12sc (12 sts)
Rnd 7 (inc, 3sc) three times (15 sts)
Rnd 8–Rnd 9 15sc (15 sts)
Rnd 10 (inc, 4sc) three times (18 sts)
Rnd 11–Rnd 13 18sc (18 sts)
Rnd 14 (inc, 5sc) three times (21 sts)
Rnd 15–Rnd 17 21sc (21 sts)
Rnd 18 9sc, inc, 1sc, inc, 9sc (23 sts)
Rnd 19 11sc, 3in1, 11sc (25 sts)
Rnd 20 2sc, (inc, 4sc) four times, inc, 2sc (30 sts)
Rnd 21 (inc, 4sc) six times (36 sts)
Rnd 22 36sc (36 sts)
Rnd 23 (11sc, inc) three times (39 sts)
Rnd 24 6sc, (inc, 12sc) twice, inc, 6sc (42 sts)
Rnd 25 (13sc, inc) three times (45 sts)
Rnd 26–Rnd 37 45sc (45 sts)
Rnd 38 7sc, dec, (13sc, dec) twice, 6sc (42 sts)
Rnd 39 42sc (42 sts)
Rnd 40 dec, 6sc, dec, 24sc, dec, 6sc (39 sts)
Rnd 41 3sc, dec, 5sc, dec, 23sc, dec, 2sc (36 sts)
Rnd 42 36sc (36 sts)

Start stuffing and continue adding more as you go.

Rnd 43 (4sc, dec) twice, 12sc, (dec, 4sc) twice (32 sts)
Rnd 44 1sc, dec, (3sc, dec) twice, 6sc, (dec, 3sc) twice, dec, 1sc (26 sts)

Rnd 45 6sc, dec, 10sc, dec, 6sc (24 sts)
Rnd 46 dec, 2sc, dec, 14sc, dec, 2sc (21 sts)
Rnd 47 21sc (21 sts)
Rnd 48 dec, 19sc (20 sts)
Rnd 49 20sc (20 sts)
Rnd 50 1sc, dec, 15sc, dec (18 sts)
Rnd 51 6hdc, 8sc, 3hdc, 1sc (18 sts)

Fasten off, leaving a piece of yarn for sewing.

Back leg (make 2):
Starting at the foot

Ch2

Rnd 1 6sc in 2nd ch from the hook (6 sts)
Rnd 2 inc six times (12 sts)
Rnd 3 inc three times, 3in1, 1sc, 3in1, inc three times, 3sc (22 sts)
Rnd 4 3sc, inc, (5sc, inc) twice, 6sc (25 sts)

Rnd 5 6sc, 10hdc, 9sc (25 sts)

Rnd 6 25sc (25 sts)

Rnd 7 5sc, (dec, 2sc) four times, 4sc (21 sts)

Rnd 8 6sc, (dec, 1sc) three times, 6sc (18 sts)

Rnd 9 (1sc, dec) six times (12 sts)

Stuff the foot and continue adding more stuffing as you go.

Rnd 10–Rnd 11 12sc (12 sts)

Rnd 12 4sc, inc, 1sc, inc, 5sc (14 sts)

Rnd 13–Rnd 14 14sc (14 sts)

Rnd 15 (6sc, inc) twice (16 sts)

Rnd 16 (7sc, inc) twice (18 sts)

Rnd 17 (2sc, inc) six times (24 sts)

Rnd 18–Rnd 19 24sc (24 sts)

Rnd 20 (2sc, dec) six times (18 sts)

Rnd 21 (1sc, dec) six times (12 sts)

Rnd 22 dec six times (6 sts)

Fasten off, leaving a piece of yarn for sewing. Sew the opening closed.

Arm (make 2):

Starting at the "hand"

Ch2

Rnd 1 6sc in 2nd ch from the hook (6 sts)

Rnd 2 inc six times (12 sts)

Rnd 3 (3sc, inc) three times (15 sts)

Rnd 4–Rnd 6 15sc (15 sts)

Rnd 7 (dec, 1sc) three times, 6sc (12 sts)

Stuff the arm and continue adding more stuffing as you go.

Rnd 8–Rnd 15 12sc (12 sts)

Rnd 16 (2sc, dec) three times (9 sts)

Rnd 17 (1sc, dec) three times (6 sts)

Fasten off, leaving a piece of yarn for sewing. Sew the opening closed.

Assembling:

Attach the legs and arms on both sides of the body approx. between rounds 24 & 25 (back legs sts) and 43 & 44 (arms sts). If you want the legs to be movable, make sure that the yarn end is pulled out on the side of the leg, 1–2 rounds below the opening. Next, insert the needle in the body and through to the other side. Be careful to go between the stitches rather than through them. Take the other limb and run the needle through it. Then, insert the needle to the body exactly in the same place where it came from. Repeat with the yarn end from the other leg.

Sew the head to the body.

Tyrannosaurus rex

Materials:

Yarn
Cotton-ish by Vickie Howell for Bernat,
70g balls, each approx. 282yd/258m

• 1 skein in Seersucker

Hook
Size C (2.75mm)

Other
6mm safety eyes

TIP
You can try adding some felt teeth for a scarier look.

Head:

Starting at the top

Ch8

Rnd 1 working on both sides of the ch: 1sc in 2nd ch from the hook, 5sc, 4in1, 5sc, inc (17 sts)

Rnd 2 inc, 5sc, inc four times, 5sc, inc twice (24 sts)

Rnd 3 1sc, inc, 5sc, (inc, 1sc) four times, 5sc, (1sc, inc) twice (31 sts)

Rnd 4 inc, 7sc, (2sc, inc) four times, 5sc, (inc, 2sc) twice (38 sts)

Rnd 5 3sc, inc, 5sc, (inc, 3sc) four times, 5sc, (3sc, inc) twice (45 sts)

Rnd 6 inc, 9sc, (4sc, inc) four times, 5sc, (inc, 4sc) twice (52 sts)

Rnd 7 18sc, inc, 6sc, inc, 26sc (54 sts)

Rnd 8–Rnd 10 54sc (54 sts)

Rnd 11 7sc, dec, 31sc, dec, 12sc (52 sts)

Rnd 12 52sc (52 sts)

Rnd 13 6sc, sc3tog, 29sc, sc3tog, 11sc (48 sts)

Rnd 14 13sc, (dec, 1sc) six times, 17sc (42 sts)

Rnd 15 (dec, 1sc) three times, 3sc, dec seven times, 3sc, (1sc, dec) four times, 1sc (28 sts)

Insert safety eyes between rounds 9 & 10, symmetrically on both sides of the head. Start stuffing and continue adding more as you go.

Rnd 16 5sc, (dec, 1sc) twice, dec twice, (1sc, dec) twice, 7sc (22 sts)

Rnd 17 4sc, (dec, 1sc) three times, dec, 7sc (18 sts)

Fasten off, leaving a long piece of yarn for sewing.

Body:

Starting at the bottom

Ch2

Rnd 16 sc in 2nd ch from the hook (6 sts)

Rnd 2 inc six times (12 sts)

Rnd 3 (1sc, inc) sts) six times (18 sts)

Rnd 4 (2sc, inc) six times (24 sts)

Rnd 5 (3sc, inc) six times (30 sts)

Rnd 6 (4sc, inc) six times (36 sts)

Rnd 7 (5sc, inc) six times (42 sts)

Rnd 8 7sc, ch6, sk5, 30sc (37 + chsp)

Rnd 9 7sc, 1sc in each of the next 2ch, dec over the next 2ch, 1sc in next 2 ch, 30sc (42 sts)

Rnd 10–Rnd 12 42sc (42 sts)

Rnd 13 (5sc, dec) twice, 28sc (40 sts)

Rnd 14 40sc (40 sts)

Rnd 22 30sc (30 sts)
Rnd 23 4sc, dec, (8sc, dec) twice, 4sc (27 sts)
Rnd 24 27sc (27 sts)
Rnd 25 (dec, 7sc) three times (24 sts)
Rnd 26 24sc (24 sts)
Rnd 27 3sc, dec, (6sc, dec) twice, 3sc (21 sts)
Rnd 28 21sc (21 sts)
Rnd 29 (dec, 5sc) three times (18 sts)
Rnd 30–Rnd 32 18sc (18 sts)

Make 1sl in the next sc and fasten off.

Tail:

Join yarn to the first sc skipped in round 8, ch 1.

Rnd 1 (inc, 1sc) twice, inc (8), inc in the side of sc (2), 1sc in each ch (6), inc in the side of sc (2) (18 sts)
Rnd 2–Rnd 6 18sc (18 sts)
Rnd 7 (dec, 4sc) three times (15 sts)
Rnd 8–Rnd 9 15sc (15 sts)
Rnd 10 dec, 13sc (14 sts)
Rnd 11 1sc, dec, 9sc, dec (12 sts)

Stuff lightly and continue as you go.

Rnd 12 12sc (12 sts)
Rnd 13 dec, 7sc, dec, 1sc (10 sts)
Rnd 14 10sc (10 sts)
Rnd 15 (1sc, dec) three times, 1sc (7 sts)
Rnd 16 dec, 1sc, dec, leave the reunworked (3 sts)

Leg (make 2):

Ch2

Rnd 1 6sc in 2nd ch from the hook (6 sts)
Rnd 2 inc six times (12 sts)
Rnd 3 (1sc, inc) six times (18 sts)
Rnd 4 (inc, 8sc) twice (20 sts)
Rnd 5–Rnd 7 20sc (20 sts)
Rnd 8 dec, 6sc, dec twice, 6sc, dec (16 sts)

Stuff lightly and continue as you go.

Rnd 9 dec, 4sc, dec twice, 4sc, dec (12 sts)

Rnd 15 (5sc, dec) twice, 26sc (38 sts)
Rnd 16 38sc (38 sts)
Rnd 17 (5sc, dec) twice, 24sc (36 sts)
Rnd 18 36sc (36 sts)
Rnd 19 5sc, dec, (10sc, dec) twice, 5sc (33 sts)
Rnd 20 33sc (33 sts)
Rnd 21 (dec, 9sc) three times (30 sts)

Rnd 10–Rnd 12 12sc (12 sts)

Rnd 13 ch4, 1sc in 2nd ch from the hook and in each of the next ch, 1sc in the next sc (first from the previous round sts) and in each of the next sts (12), now you'll work on the other side of the first ch: 1sc in each of the first 2 ch, inc in the last ch - new beginning of the round–move your marker if you're using one (19 sts)

Rnd 14 inc, 16sc, inc twice (22 sts)

Rnd 15–Rnd 16 22sc (22 sts)

Rnd 17 dec, 5sc, dec three times, 5sc, dec twice (16 sts)

Rnd 18 dec, 2sc, dec three times, 2sc, dec twice (10 sts)

Fasten off, leaving a long piece of yarn for sewing. Sew the opening closed (flat). Pull the yarn end to the upper part of the leg (between rounds 4 & 5 sts) to sew it to the body–it'll flatten the sole at the same time.

Arm (make 2):

Ch2

Rnd 1 6sc in 2nd ch from the hook (6 sts)

Rnd 2 inc six times (12 sts)

Rnd 3 (inc, 5sc) twice (14 sts)

Rnd 4–Rnd 5 14sc (14 sts)

Rnd 6 dec, 3sc, dec twice, 3sc, dec (10 sts)

Rnd 7 10sc (10 sts)

Rnd 8 4sc, dec, 4sc (9 sts)

Stuff lightly and continue adding more as you go.

Rnd 9 3sc, sc3tog, 3sc (7 sts)

Rnd 10–Rnd 11 7sc (7 sts)

Rnd 12 1sc, inc, 3sc, inc, 1sc (9 sts)

Rnd 13 9sc (9 sts)

Rnd 14 (dec, 1sc) three times (6 sts)

Fasten off, leaving a long piece of yarn for sewing. Pull the yarn end to the upper part of the arm (between rounds 3 & 4 sts) to sew it to the body.

Assembling:

Attach the legs and arms on both sides of the body approx. between rounds 7 & 8 (legs sts) and 22 & 23 (arms sts).

If you want the legs to be movable, make sure that the yarn end is pulled out on the side of the leg, 1–2 rounds below the opening. Next, insert the needle in the body and through to the other side. Be careful to go between the stitches rather than through them. Take the other limb and run the needle through it. Then, insert the needle into the body exactly in the same place where it came from. Repeat with the yarn end from the other leg. Sew the head to the body.

Tropeognathus

Materials:

Yarn
Cotton-ish by Vickie Howell for Bernat,
70g balls, each approx. 282yd/258m

- 1 skein in Spinning Jenny

Hook
Size C (2.75mm)

Other
4.5mm safety eyes

TIP
You can block and stiffen the wings with starch if you don't want them to be wavy.

Wing (make 2):

Ch2

Row 1 1sc in 2nd ch from the hook, ch1, turn (1 sts)

Row 2 inc, ch1, turn (2 sts)

Row 3 inc twice, , ch1, turn (4 sts)

Row 4 inc, 3sc, ch1, turn (5 sts)

Row 5 4sc, inc, ch1, turn (6 sts)

Row 6 inc, 5sc, ch1, turn (7 sts)

Row 7 6sc, inc, ch1, turn (8 sts)

Row 8 inc, 7sc, ch1, turn (9 sts)

Row 9 8sc, inc, ch1, turn (10 sts)

Row 10 inc, 9sc, ch1, turn (11 sts)

Row 11 10sc, inc, ch1, turn (12 sts)

Row 12 inc, 11sc, ch1, turn (13 sts)

Row 13 12sc, inc, ch1, turn (14 sts)

Row 14 inc, 13sc, ch1, turn (15 sts)

Row 15 14sc, inc, ch1, turn (16 sts)

Row 16 inc, 15sc, ch1, turn (17 sts)

Row 17 16sc, inc, ch1, turn (18 sts)

Row 18 inc, 17sc, ch1, turn (19 sts)

Row 19 18sc, inc, ch1, turn (20 sts)

Row 20 inc, 19sc, ch1, turn (21 sts)

Row 21 20sc, inc, ch1, turn (22 sts)

Row 22 inc, 21sc, ch1, turn (23 sts)

Row 23 22sc, inc, ch1, turn (24 sts)

Row 24 inc, 23sc, ch1, turn (25 sts)

Row 25 24sc, inc, ch1, turn (26 sts)

Row 26 inc, 25sc, ch1, turn (27 sts)

Row 27 26sc, inc, ch1, turn (28 sts)

Row 28 inc, 27sc, ch1, <u>don't</u> turn (29 sts)

You'll be now working in the side of the rows, in the upper part of the wing, to create the arm and fingers.

Make 1sc in each row from 28 to 16 (12sts). Now we'll make the fingers: (ch3, 1sl in the 2nd ch from the hook and in the next ch) three times, 1sl in the last sc made (3 fingers made), turn. Now make 1sl in each of the sc to go back to the beginning.

Fasten off, leaving a long piece of yarn for sewing.

You may want to block the wings before sewing them to the body.

Legs and body
Leg:

Starting at the foot

Ch2

Rnd 1 6sc in 2nd ch from the hook (6 sts)

Rnd 3 15sc, inc, 2sc, inc, 15sc (36 sts)

Rnd 4 3sc, (inc, 5sc) twice, inc, ch5, sk5, (inc, 5sc) twice, inc, 2sc (37 +ch-5-sp sts)

Rnd 5 19sc, 1sc in each ch (not in chsp sts), 18sc (42 sts)

Rnd 6–Rnd 10 42sc (42 sts)

At this point you may want to make the claws and tail, as it'll be easier to weave in and secure the ends this way—you have access to the inside of the body and you can tie the ends together easily. You can, however, choose to make these at the very end and continue with the body.

Rnd 11 (12sc, dec) three times (39 sts)

Rnd 12–Rnd 13 39sc (39 sts)

Rnd 14 6sc, (dec, 11sc) twice, dec, 5sc (36 sts)

Rnd 15–Rnd 16 36sc (36 sts)

Start stuffing and continue as you go. Tail and legs don't require stuffing.

Rnd 17 (10sc, dec) three times (33 sts)

Rnd 18–Rnd 19 33sc (33 sts)

Rnd 20 5sc, (dec, 9sc) twice, dec, 4sc (30 sts)

Rnd 21–Rnd 22 30sc (30 sts)

Rnd 23 (8sc, dec) three times (27 sts)

Rnd 24–Rnd 25 27sc (27 sts)

Rnd 26 4sc, (dec, 7sc) twice, dec, 3sc (24 sts)

Rnd 27–Rnd 28 24sc (24 sts)

Rnd 29 (6sc, dec) three times (21 sts)

Rnd 30–Rnd 31 21sc (21 sts)

Rnd 32 3sc, (dec, 5sc) twice, dec, 2sc (18 sts)

Rnd 33–Rnd 24 18sc (18 sts)

Fasten off.

Toes/Claws:

Join yarn to the first FL left in round 2.

Rnd 1 *ch3, 1sl in 2nd ch from the hook and in the next st, 1sl to the next FL*, rep from * to * once, ch3, 1sl in 2dn ch from the hook and in the next st, 1sl to the next FL, 1sl to the 3rd FL again.

Fasten off, weave in the ends.

Rnd 2 2sc, in BLO: 3sc, 1sc (6 sts)

Rnd 3–Rnd 4 6sc (6 sts)

Rnd 5 (2sc, inc) twice (8 sts) Mark the 6th stitch of the round.

Fasten off. Make the second leg just like the first one, but don't fasten off. We'll now join them and start the body. Starting in the marked on the first leg:

Rnd 1 inc, 2sc, inc twice, 2sc, 3in1, move to the sts from the second leg, 3in1, 2sc, inc twice, 2sc, inc (26 sts)

Rnd 2 1sc, inc, (2sc, inc) three times, 4sc, inc, (2sc, inc) three times, 1sc (34 sts)

Tail:

Join yarn to the first skipped in round 4, ch 1.

Rnd 1 1sc in each skipped in round 4 (5), 1sc in the side of sc (1), 1sc in each chain (5) and 1sc in the side of sc (1) (12 sts)

Rnd 2 12sc (12 sts)

Rnd 3 (4sc, dec) twice (10 sts)

Rnd 4 (3sc, dec) twice (8 sts)

Rnd 5 (2sc, dec) twice (6 sts)

Rnd 6 (1sc, dec) twice (4 sts)

Fasten off, sew the opening closed by pulling the yarn through all FL of the last round. Weave in the end.

Head:

Starting at the nose

Ch2

Rnd 1 6sc in 2nd ch from the hook (6 sts)

Rnd 2 inc six times (12 sts)

Rnd 3 inc, 1sc, inc, 3sc, inc three times, 3sc (17 sts)

Rnd 4 2sc, 3in1, 7sc, 3in1 twice, 5sc (23 sts)

Rnd 5 2sc, inc, 1sc, inc, 8sc, inc, 2sc, inc, 6sc (27 sts)

Rnd 6 16sc, (inc, 1sc) twice, inc, 6sc (30 sts)

Rnd 7–Rnd 11 30sc (30 sts)

Rnd 12 17sc, (dec, 1sc) twice, dec, 5sc (27 sts)

Rnd 13 3sc, dec, 1sc, dec, 8sc, dec, 2sc, dec, 5sc (23 sts)

Rnd 14 3sc, sc3tog, 7sc, sc3tog twice, 4sc (17 sts)

Stuff and continue as you go.

Rnd 15–Rnd 20 17sc (17 sts)

Rnd 21 4sc, inc, 7sc, inc twice, 3sc (20 sts)

Rnd 22 20sc (20 sts)

Rnd 23 (3sc, inc) five times (25 sts)

Rnd 24 1sc, (inc, 4sc) four times, inc, 3sc (30 sts)

Rnd 25 (4sc, inc) six times (36 sts)

Rnd 26 36sc (36 sts)

Rnd 27 26sc, inc, 1sc, inc, 7sc (38 sts)

Rnd 28 28sc, 3in1, 9sc (40 sts)

Rnd 29–Rnd 33 40sc (40 sts)

Insert safety eyes between rounds 25 & 26, about 8 stitches apart.

Rnd 24 (6sc, dec) five times (35 sts)

Rnd 35 2sc, (dec, 5sc) four times, dec, 3sc (30 sts)

Rnd 36 (dec, 3sc) six times (24 sts)

Rnd 37 (2sc, dec) six times (18 sts)

Rnd 28 (1sc, dec) six times (12 sts)

Rnd 29 dec six times (6 sts)

Fasten off, sew the opening closed.

Assembling:

Attach the wings on both sides of the body. Sew the head to the body.

44

Edmontosaurus

Materials:

Yarn

Cotton-ish by Vickie Howell for Bernat, 70g balls, each approx. 282yd/258m

- 1 skein in Cotton Harvest

Hook

Size C (2.75mm)

Other

4.5mm safety eyes

TIP

You can make the spikes in a contrasting color to make them pop.

Head, body and tail:
Starting at the head

Ch2

Rnd 1 6sc in 2nd ch from the hook (6sts)
Rnd 2 inc six times (12sts)
Rnd 3 4sc, inc three times, 5sc (15sts)
Rnd 4 15sc (15sts)
Rnd 5 5sc, (inc, 1sc) three times, 4sc (18sts)
Rnd 6 18sc (18sts)
Rnd 7 5sc, inc, (2sc, inc) twice, 6sc, (21sts)
Rnd 8 21sc (21sts)
Rnd 9 (inc, 2sc) twice, 12sc, inc, 2sc (24sts)
Rnd 10 24sc (24sts)
Rnd 11 (3sc, inc) six times (30sts)
Rnd 12 1sc, (inc, 4sc) five times, inc, 3sc (36sts)
Rnd 13–Rnd 14 36sc (36sts)
Rnd 15 (4sc, dec) six times (30sts)

Insert safety eyes between rounds 9 & 10, on both sides of the muzzle. Start stuffing and continue adding more as you go.

Rnd 16 30sc (30sts)
Rnd 17 (3sc, dec) six times (24sts)
Rnd 18 9sc, (dec, 2sc) three times, 3sc (21sts)
Rnd 19 10sc, (dec, 1sc) three times, 2sc (18sts)
Rnd 20 18sc (18sts)

Rnd 21 (1hdc, hdc inc) three times, 2sc, dec, (1sc, dec) twice, 2sc (18sts)
Rnd 22 5sc, hdc inc twice, 6sc, sc3tog, 2sc (18sts)
Rnd 23 18sc (18sts)
Rnd 24 (2sc, inc) six times (24sts)
Rnd 25 1sc, (inc, 3sc) five times, inc, 2sc (30sts)
Rnd 26 (4sc, inc) six times (36sts)
Rnd 27 13sc, inc, 1sc, inc, 15sc, inc, 1sc, inc, 2sc (40sts)
Rnd 28 15sc, 3in1, 24sc (42sts)
Rnd 29–Rnd 30 42sc (42sts)
Rnd 31 12sc, inc, 7sc, inc, 16sc, inc, 4sc (45sts)
Rnd 32–Rnd 46 45sc (45sts)
Rnd 47 (13sc, dec) three times (42sts)
Rnd 48 42sc (42sts)
Rnd 49 10sc, (dec, 8sc) twice, dec, 10sc (39sts)
Rnd 50 39sc (39sts)
Rnd 51 14sc, dec, 7sc, dec, 14sc (37sts)
Rnd 52 10sc, (dec, 6sc) twice, dec, 9sc (34sts)

Spikes:

Starting at round 15, work 42 surface chains down the dinosaur's spine, ch1, turn. Working in the chains:

Rnd 1 1hdc, *1sl st, [1sl st, ch1, 1hdc] in the next ch,* rep from * to * till the last, 1sl in the last ch.

Front leg (make 2):
Starting at the foot

Ch2

Rnd 1 6sc in 2nd ch from the hook (6sts)
Rnd 2 inc six times (12sts)
Rnd 3 3sc, (inc, 1sc) three times, 3sc (15sts)
Rnd 4 In BLO: 15sc (15sts)
Rnd 5 15sc (15sts)
Rnd 6 5sc, dec three times, 4sc (12sts)

Start stuffing and continue adding more as you go.

Rnd 53 13sc, dec, 5sc, dec, 12sc (32sts)
Rnd 54 9sc, (dec, 4sc) twice, dec, 9sc (29sts)
Rnd 55 11sc, dec, 3sc, dec, 11sc (27sts)
Rnd 56 6sc, (dec, 5sc) three times (24sts)
Rnd 57 24sc (24sts)
Rnd 58 10sc, dec, 1sc, dec, 9sc (22sts)
Rnd 57 7sc, dec, 5sc, dec, 6sc (20sts)
Rnd 58 9sc, sc3tog, 8sc (18sts)
Rnd 59 18sc (18sts)
Rnd 60 6sc, dec, 3sc, dec, 5sc (16sts)
Rnd 61 16sc (16sts)
Rnd 62 7sc, sc3tog, 6sc (14sts)
Rnd 63 14sc (14sts)
Rnd 64 4sc, dec, 3sc, dec, 3sc (12sts)
Rnd 65 12sc (12sts)
Rnd 66 6sc, sc3tog, 3sc (10sts)
Rnd 67 10sc (10sts)
Rnd 68 (3sc, dec) twice (8sts)
Rnd 69 8sc (8sts)
Rnd 70 (2sc, dec) twice (6sts)
Rnd 71 (1sc, dec) twice (4sts)

Rnd 7–Rnd 17 12sc (12sts)
Rnd 18 dec six times (6sts)

Fasten off, leaving a piece of yarn for sewing.

Back leg (make 2):
Starting at the foot

Ch2

Rnd 1 6sc in 2nd ch from the hook (6sts)
Rnd 2 inc six times (12sts)
Rnd 3 (1sc, inc) twice *[ch1, 1hdc, ch1] in the next st, inc*, rep twice more, 1sc, inc
Rnd 4 in BLO: 6sc, *hdc3tog (place hook in front loops of ch 1, hdc and ch1 from the previous round sts), 2sc* rep twice more, 3sc in BLO (18sts)
Rnd 5 7sc, (dec, 1sc) twice, dec, 3sc (15sts)
Rnd 6–Rnd 7 15sc (15sts)
Rnd 8 (3sc, dec) three times (12sts)

Start stuffing and continue adding more as you go.

Rnd 9–Rnd 12 12sc (12sts)

Rnd 13 2sc, 3in1, 5sc, 3in1, 3sc (16sts)
Rnd 14 3sc, inc, 7sc, inc, 4sc (18sts)
Rnd 15–Rnd 17 18sc (18sts)
Rnd 18 (1sc, dec) six times (12sts)
Rnd 19 dec six times (6sts)
Fasten off, leaving a piece of yarn for sewing.

Assembling:

Attach the legs on both sides of the body approx. between rounds 31 & 32 and 47 & 48. If you want the legs to be movable,

make sure that the yarn end is pulled out on the side of the leg, 1-2 rounds below the opening. Next, insert the needle in the body and through to the other side. Be careful to go between the stitches rather than through them. Take the other limb and run the needle through it. Then, insert the needle into the body exactly in the same place where it came from. Repeat with the yarn end from the other leg.

Triceratops

Materials:

Yarn

Cotton-ish by Vickie Howell for Bernat,
70g balls, each approx. 282yd/258m

- 1 skein in Jade Jersey
- 1 skein in Cotton Field

Hook

Size C (2.75mm sts)

Other

6mm safety eyes

TIP

You can try attaching the head using a plastic joint, so that it rotates.

Insert safety eyes between rounds 12 & 13 (about 9 sts apart). Start stuffing and continue adding more as you go.

Rnd 22 20sc, dec, 3sc, dec, 21sc (46 sts)
Rnd 23 17sc, dec, 7sc, dec, 18sc (44 sts)
Rnd 24 14sc, dec, 11sc, dec, 15sc (42 sts)
Rnd 25 (5sc, dec) six times (36 sts)
Rnd 26 2sc, (dec, 4sc) five times, dec, 2sc (30 sts)
Rnd 27 (3sc, dec) six times (24 sts)
Rnd 28 1sc, (dec, 2sc) five times, dec, 1sc (18 sts)
Rnd 29 (dec, 1sc) six times (12 sts)
Rnd 30 dec six times (6 sts)

Fasten off leaving a piece of yarn for sewing.

Frill:

Join yarn to the firloop left in round 19, ch 1.
Row 1 (inc, 4sc) three times, inc, 1sc, inc, (4sc, inc) three times, ch1, turn (41 sts)
Row 2 inc, (19sc, inc) twice, ch1, turn (44 sts)
Row 3–Row 5 44sc, ch1, turn (44 sts)
Row 6 21sc, inc, 22sc (45 sts)

Change color to CC.

Row 1 ch2, 2dc in the first, (sk1, 2sc, ch1, 3dc in 1) x10, sk1, 2sc, ch1, [2dc, ch1, 1sl st] in the last

Horns—big (make 2):

With CC, ch2
Rnd 1 4sc in 2nd ch from the hook (4 sts)
Rnd 2 (inc, 1sc) twice (6 sts)
Rnd 3 (inc, 1sc) three times (9 sts)
Rnd 4 – Rnd 7 9sc (9)

Make 1sl st, fasten off, leaving a long piece of yarn for sewing. Stuff lightly.

Horn—small:

With CC, ch2
Rnd 1 4sc in 2nd ch from the hook (4 sts)
Rnd 2 (inc, 1sc) twice (6 sts)

Head:

Starting at the nose

Ch2
Rnd 1 6sc in 2nd ch from the hook (6 sts)
Rnd 2 inc six times (12 sts)
Rnd 3 (1sc, inc) six times (18 sts)
Rnd 4 (inc, 2sc) six times (24 sts)
Rnd 5 3sc, inc, (7sc, inc) twice, 4sc (27 sts)
Rnd 6–Rnd 11 27sc
Rnd 12 10sc, (inc, 1sc) twice, inc, 12sc (30 sts)
Rnd 13 9sc, (inc, 2sc) three times, inc, 11sc (34 sts)
Rnd 14 8sc, (inc, 3sc) four times, inc, 9sc (39 sts)
Rnd 15–Rnd 16 39sc (39 sts)
Rnd 17 10sc, inc, (6sc, inc) twice, 14sc (42 sts)
Rnd 18 42sc (42 sts)
Rnd 19 (6sc, inc) six times (48 sts)
Rnd 20 48sc (48 sts)
Rnd 21 7sc, 33sc in BLO, 8sc (48 sts)

Rnd 3 (inc, 1sc) three times (9 sts)

Make 1sl st, fasten off, leaving a long piece of yarn for sewing. Stuff lightly.

Body:

Starting at the top

Ch16

Rnd 1 working on both sides of the chain:
2sc in 2nd ch from the hook, 13sc, 4in1, 13sc, inc (34 sts)

Rnd 2 inc twice, 13sc, inc four times, 13sc, inc twice (42 sts)

Rnd 3 (1sc, inc) twice, 13sc, (1sc, inc) four times, 13sc, (1sc, inc) twice (50 sts)

Rnd 4 1sc, inc, 2sc, inc, 15sc, (inc, 2sc) four times, 13sc, inc, 2sc, inc, 1sc (58 sts)

Rnd 5 (3sc, inc) twice, 13sc, (inc, 3sc) four times, 13sc, (3sc, inc) twice (66 sts)

Rnd 6 2sc, inc, 4sc, inc, 17sc, (inc, 4sc) four times, 13sc, inc, 4sc, inc, 2sc (74 sts)

Rnd 7 (5sc, inc) twice, 13sc, (inc, 5sc) four times, 13sc, (5sc, inc) twice (82 sts)

Rnd 8 82sc (82 sts)

Rnd 9 39sc, ch7, sk7, 36sc (75 + ch-7-sp)

Rnd 10 38sc, dec (over sc and ch), 5sc, dec (over ch and sc), 35sc (80 sts)

Rnd 11–Rnd 17 80sc (80 sts)

Rnd 18 (5sc, dec) twice, 13sc, (5sc, dec) four times, 18sc, dec, 5sc (73 sts)

Rnd 19 dec, 4sc, ch10, sk8, 13sc, sk8, ch10, 2sc, sc3tog, 2sc, sk8, ch10, 13sc, sk8, ch10, 2sc (38sc + 4 ch-10-sp)

Rnd 20 3sc, dec twice, 6sc, dec twice, 9sc, dec twice, 6sc, dec twice, 1sc, dec twice, 6sc, dec twice, 9sc, dec twice, 6sc, dec twice (62 sts)

Rnd 21 sc3tog, dec twice, 3sc, dec, 11sc, dec, 3sc, dec twice, 1sc, dec twice, 3sc, dec, 11sc, dec, 3sc, dec twice (48 sts)

Rnd 22 dec twice, (2sc, dec) five times, dec twice, (2sc, dec) five times (34 sts)

Stuff the body and continue adding more as you go.

Rnd 23 dec three times, 5sc, dec seven times, 5sc, dec twice (22 sts)

Rnd 24 dec, 6sc, dec, 1sc, dec, 6sc, dec, 1sc (18 sts)

Fasten off, sew the opening closed.

Leg (make 4):

Join yarn the first sc skipped in round 19 (in any of the holes—we'll create one leg in each), Ch1

Rnd 1 1sc in every sc (8), 1sc in the side of sc (1), 1sc in each ch (10), 1sc in the side of sc (1) (20 sts)
Rnd 2–Rnd 6 20sc (20 sts)
Rnd 7 in BLO: (2sc, dec) five times (15 sts)

Start stuffing and continue adding more as you go.

Rnd 8 (dec twice, 1sc) three times (9 sts)
Rnd 9 dec twice, leave the reunworked

Fasten off, sew the opening closed.

Toes:

Mark 5 loops in front of every leg (we left them free in round 7)—we'll be making toes in them. Join CC to the firstitch, ch1

Rnd 1 [1sc, 1sl st] in the first loop, 1sl in the next loop, [1sc, 1sl st] in the next loop, 1sl in the next loop, [1sc, 1sl st] in the last loop

Fasten off, sew the opening closed.

Tail:

Join yarn the first sc skipped in round 9, ch 1.

Rnd 1 1sc in every sc (7), 1sc in the side of sc (1), 1sc in each ch (7), 1sc in the side of sc (1) (16 sts)
Rnd 2 3sc, dec, 6sc, inc, 4sc (16 sts)
Rnd 3 2sc, sc3tog, 4sc, inc, 1sc, inc, 4sc (16 sts)
Rnd 4 16sc (16 sts)
Rnd 5 (dec, 1sc) twice, 10sc (14 sts)
Rnd 6–Rnd 7 14sc (14 sts)
Rnd 8 (5sc, dec) twice (12 sts)
Rnd 9 12sc (12 sts)

Start stuffing and continue adding more as you go.

Rnd 10 (2sc, dec) three times (9 sts)
Rnd 11 9sc (9 sts)
Rnd 12 (1sc, dec) three times (6 sts)
Rnd 13 dec twice, leave the rest unworked

Fasten off, sew the opening closed.

Assembling:

Sew the horns on the head—bigger ones between round 18 and the frill and the small one between rounds 5 & 7, in the center of the nose. Attach the head at approx. round 2.

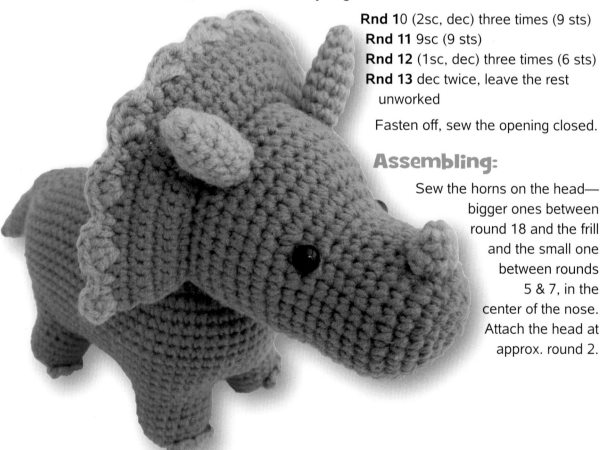

Elasmosaurus

Materials:

Yarn
Cotton-ish by Vickie Howell for Bernat,
70g balls, each approx. 282yd/258m

- 1 skein in Lemon Twill

Hook
Size C (2.75mm)

Other
2 4.5mm safety eyes

TIP
You can insert
a pipe cleaner
in the dinosaur's
neck to make
it poseable.

Head, body and tail:
Starting at the head

Ch2

Rnd 1 6sc in 2nd ch from the hook (6 sts)
Rnd 2 (1sc, inc) three times (9 sts)
Rnd 3 (2sc, inc) three times (12 sts)
Rnd 4 (3sc, inc) three times (15 sts)
Rnd 5 (4sc, inc) three times (18 sts)
Rnd 6–8 18sc (18 sts)
Rnd 9 inc, 2sc, inc, (1sc, inc) three times, 2sc, inc, 5sc (24 sts)
Rnd 10 24sc (24 sts)
Rnd 11 3sc, inc, (4sc, inc) twice, 10sc (27sts)
Rnd 12–14 27sc (27 sts)
Rnd 15 3sc, dec, (6sc, dec) twice, 6sc (24 sts)
Rnd 16 24sc (24 sts)

Insert safety eyes between rounds 9 and 10 about 9 sts apart. Start stuffing and continue adding more as you go.

Rnd 17 (2sc, dec) six times (18 sts)
Rnd 18 18sc (18 sts)
Rnd 19 4sc, dec, (1sc, dec) twice, 6sc (15 sts)
Rnd 20–45 15sc (15 sts)
Rnd 46 1sc, inc, (2sc, inc) twice, 7sc (18 sts)
Rnd 47 (inc, 2sc) six times (24 sts)
Rnd 48 4sc, 3in1, 9sc, 3in1, 6sc, 3in1, 2sc (30 sts)
Rnd 49 (4sc, inc) six times (36 sts)
Rnd 50 6sc, 3in1, 13sc, 3in1, 10sc, 3in1, 4sc (42 sts)
Rnd 51 42sc (42 sts)
Rnd 52 1sc, inc, 27sc, inc, 12sc (44 sts)
Rnd 53 39sc, 3in1, 4sc (46 sts)
Rnd 54 9sc, inc, 15sc, inc, 20sc (48 sts)
Rnd 55–72 48sc (48 sts)
Rnd 73 6sc, dec, 28sc, dec, 7sc, dec, 1sc (45 sts)
Rnd 74 2sc, dec, 34sc, dec, 5sc (43 sts)

Rnd 75 8sc, dec, 20sc, dec, 8sc, dec, 1sc (40 sts)
Rnd 76 5sc, dec, 24sc, dec, 7sc (38 sts)
Rnd 77 35sc, sc3tog (36 sts)
Rnd 78 2sc, (dec, 4sc) fives times, dec, 2sc (30 sts)
Rnd 79 dec, 2sc, dec, 3sc, dec, 8sc, dec, 3sc, dec, 2sc, dec (24 sts)
Rnd 80 1sc, (dec, 2sc) five times, dec, 1sc (18 sts)
Rnd 81 18sc (18 sts)
Rnd 82 4sc, dec, 7sc, dec, 3sc (16 sts)
Rnd 83–85 16sc (16 sts)
Rnd 86 3sc, dec, 6sc, dec, 3sc (14 sts)

Rnd 87–89 14sc (14 sts)

Rnd 90 3sc, dec, 5sc, dec, 2sc (12 sts)

Rnd 91–93 12sc (12 sts)

Rnd 94 (2sc, dec) three times (9 sts)

Rnd 95–96 9sc (9 sts)

Rnd 97 (1sc, dec) three times (6 sts)

Rnd 98 6sc (6 sts)

Rnd 99 (1sc, dec) twice (4 sts)

Fasten off, sew the opening closed.

Flipper (make 4)

Ch2

Rnd 1 6sc in 2nd ch from the hook (6 sts)

Rnd 2 (1sc, inc) three times (9 sts)

Rnd 3 3in1, 8sc (11 sts)

Rnd 4 11sc (11 sts)

Rnd 5 inc, 1sc, inc, 8sc (13 sts)

Rnd 6 13sc (13 sts)

Rnd 7 2sc, 3in1, 10sc (15 sts)

Rnd 8–12 15sc (15 sts)

Rnd 13 3sc, sc3tog, 5sc, inc twice, 2sc (15 sts)

Rnd 14 2sc, sc3tog, 6sc, inc, 3sc (14 sts)

Rnd 15–16 14sc (14 sts)

Fasten off, leaving a piece of yarn for sewing.

Assembly

Sew the flippers symmetrically on both sides of the body-one pair between rounds 51 & 57 and the second pair between rounds 67 & 73.

Pterodactyl

Materials:

Yarn

Cotton-ish by Vickie Howell for Bernat, 70g balls, each approx. 282yd/258m

- 1 skein in Crimson Twine

Hook

Size C (2.75mm)

Other

6mm safety eyes

TIP

If you'd like the wings to be sturdier, you can make two more and sew them together to create the double thick layer.

Head:

Starting at the nose

Ch2

Rnd 1 6sc in 2nd ch from the hook (6 sts)
Rnd 2 (inc, 1sc) three times (9 sts)
Rnd 3 (2sc, inc) three times (12 sts)
Rnd 4 1sc, inc, (3sc, inc) twice, 2sc (15 sts)
Rnd 5 15sc (15 sts)
Rnd 6 (inc, 4sc) three times (18 sts)
Rnd 7 18sc (18 sts)
Rnd 8 (inc, 5sc) three times (21 sts)
Rnd 9 21sc (21 sts)
Rnd 10 (inc, 6sc) three times (24 sts)
Rnd 11–Rnd 13 24sc (24 sts)
Rnd 14 6sc, (inc, 1sc) six times, 6sc (30 sts)
Rnd 15 30sc (30 sts)
Rnd 16 (4sc, inc) six times (36 sts)
Rnd 17 36sc (36 sts)
Rnd 18 (5sc, inc) six times (42 sts)
Rnd 19–Rnd 21 42sc (42 sts)
Rnd 22 (dec, 3sc) three times, 12sc,
   (dec, 3sc) three times (36 sts)
Rnd 23 36sc (36 sts)

Insert safety eyes between rounds 14 & 15
Start stuffing and continue adding more as
you go.

Rnd 24 (dec, 3sc) three times, 6sc, (dec,
3sc) three times (30 sts)
Rnd 25 11sc, ch8, sk8, 11sc (22+ch-8-sp)
Rnd 26 (3sc, dec) six times (24 sts)
Rnd 27 1sc, dec, 3sc, dec, (2sc, dec)
   four times (18 sts)
Rnd 28 (dec, 1sc) six times (12 sts)
Rnd 29 dec six times (6 sts)

Fasten off, leaving a piece of yarn for
sewing. Sew the opening closed.

Crest:

Join yarn to the first sc skipped in round 25.

Rnd 1 1sc in each skipped sc (8), inc in the
   side of sc (2), 1sc in each ch (8), inc in the
   side of sc (2) (20 sts)

Rnd 2 20sc (20 sts)
Rnd 3 (8sc, dec) twice (18 sts)
Rnd 4–Rnd 5 18sc (18 sts)
Rnd 6 (4sc, dec) three times (15 sts)
Rnd 7 15sc (15 sts)
Rnd 8 2sc, (dec, 3sc) twice, dec, 1sc (12 sts)

Stuff and continue adding more as you go.

Rnd 9 12sc (12 sts)
Rnd 10 (2sc, dec) three times (9 sts)
Rnd 11 9sc (9 sts)
Rnd 12 (dec, 1sc) three times (6 sts)

Fasten off, leaving a piece of yarn for
sewing. Sew the opening closed.

Body:

Starting at the bottom

Ch2

Rnd 1 6sc in 2nd ch from the hook (6 sts)

Rnd 2 inc six times (12 sts)

Rnd 3 (1sc, inc) six times (18 sts)

Rnd 4 (inc, 2sc) six times (24 sts)

Rnd 5 2sc, (inc, 3sc) five times, inc, 1sc (30 sts)

Rnd 6 (inc, 4sc) six times (36 sts)

Rnd 7 4sc, inc, 5sc, inc, 2sc, 2sc in BLO, 1sc, inc, 1sc, 2sc in BLO sts), 2sc, (inc, 5sc) twice, inc, 1sc (42 sts)

Rnd 8–Rnd 13 42sc (42 sts)

At this point you may want to make the claws and tail, as it'll be easier to weave in and secure the ends this way—you have access to the inside of the body and you can tie the ends together easily. You can, however, choose to make these at the very end and continue with the body.

Rnd 14 (5sc, dec) six times (36 sts)

Rnd 15 36sc (36 sts)

Rnd 16 (10sc, dec) three times (33 sts)

Rnd 17 33sc (33 sts)

Rnd 18 6sc, (dec, 9sc) twice, dec, 3sc (30 sts)

Rnd 19 30sc (30 sts)

Rnd 20 (8sc, dec) three times (27 sts)

Rnd 21 27sc (27 sts)

Rnd 22 5sc, (dec, 7sc) twice, dec, 2sc (24 sts)

Start stuffing and continue adding more as you go.

Rnd 23–Rnd 24 24sc (24 sts)

Rnd 25 (6sc, dec) three times (21 sts)

Rnd 26–Rnd 27 21sc (21 sts)

Rnd 28 4sc, (dec, 5sc) twice, dec, 1sc (18 sts)

Rnd 29–Rnd 30 18sc (18 sts)

Rnd 31 5sc, dec, 8sc, dec, 1sc (16 sts)

Rnd 32 16sc (16 sts)

Rnd 33 2sc, (dec, 3sc) twice, dec, 1sc (12 sts)

Make 1sl in the next sc and fasten off, leaving a piece of yarn for sewing.

Feet:

Join yarn to one of the loops skipped in round 7, ch1

Rnd 1 1sc in the first loop, inc in the second loop, ch1, turn (3 sts)

Rnd 2 (1dc, ch2, 1sl sts) in the first sc, (1sl st, ch1, 1dc, ch2, 1sl st) in each of the next 2sc (3 toes made)

Fasten off. Repeat these two rows in the next pair of skipped loops for the second foot. Fasten off, weave in the ends.

Tail:

Ch2

Rnd 1 4sc in 2nd ch from the hook (4 sts)
Rnd 2 (inc, 1sc) twice (6 sts)
Rnd 3 (inc, 2sc) twice (8 sts)
Rnd 4 (inc, 3sc) twice (10 sts)
Rnd 5 dec, 1sc, dec twice, 1sc, dec (6 sts)
Rnd 6–**Rnd 11** 6sc in FLO (6 sts)
Rnd 12 6sc (6 sts)
Rnd 13 3sc, 3in1, 2sc (8 sts)

Fasten off, leaving a piece of yarn for sewing. Tail doesn't require stuffing.

Wing (make 2):

Ch2

Row 1 1sc in 2nd ch from the hook, turn, ch1 (1 st)
Row 2 inc, turn, ch1 (2 sts)
Row 3 1sc, inc, turn, ch1 (3 sts)
Row 4 3sc, turn, ch1 (3 sts)
Row 5 inc, 2sc, turn, ch1 (4 sts)
Row 6 4sc, turn, ch1 (4 sts)
Row 7 3sc, inc, turn, ch1 (5 sts)
Row 8 5sc, turn, ch1 (5 sts)
Row 9 4sc, inc, turn, ch1 (6 sts)
Row 10 6sc, turn, ch1 (6 sts)
Row 11 5sc, inc, turn, ch1 (7 sts)
Row 12 7sc, turn, ch1 (7 sts)
Row 13 6sc, inc, turn, ch1 (8 sts)
Row 14 8sc, turn, ch1 (8 sts)
Row 15 7sc, inc, turn, ch1 (9 sts)
Row 16 9sc, turn, ch1 (9 sts)
Row 17 8sc, 3in1, turn, ch1 (11 sts)
Row 18 11sc, turn, ch1 (11 sts)
Row 19 10sc, 3in1, turn, ch1 (13 sts)
Row 20 13sc, turn, ch1 (13 sts)
Row 21 12sc, 3in1, turn, ch1 (15 sts)
Row 22 15sc, turn, ch1 (15 sts)
Row 23 14sc, 3in1, turn, ch1 (17 sts)

Row 24 17sc, turn, ch1 (17 sts)
Row 25 16sc, 3in1, turn, ch1 (19 sts)
Row 26 19sc, turn, ch1 (19 sts)
Row 27 18sc, 3in1, turn, ch1 (21 sts)
Row 28 21sc, turn, ch1 (21 sts)
Row 29 20sc, 3in1, turn, ch1 (23 sts)
Row 30 23sc, turn, ch1 (23 sts)
Row 31 21sc, 3in1, turn, ch1 (25 sts)
Row 32 25sc, turn, ch1 (25 sts)

Fasten off, leaving a piece of yarn for sewing.

Hand:

Join yarn at the top of the wing around row 18, ch 1.

Row 1 1sc in each of the next 3 rows, ch1, turn (3 sts)

Row 2 (1dc, ch2, 1sl st) in the first sc, (1sl st, ch1, 1dc, ch2, 1sl st) in each of the next 2sc (3 fingers made)

Fasten off, weave in the ends.

Assembling:

Sew the head to the body. Attach the wings on both sides of the body. Sew the tail at the back.

Parasaurolophus

Materials:

Yarn

Cotton-ish by Vickie Howell for Bernat,
70g balls, each approx. 282yd/258m

- 1 skein in Cotton Field

Hook

Size C (2.75mm)

Other

6mm safety eyes

TIP

Since the head crest is attached later and not worked together with the head, you can easily change its color to a contrasting one if you'd like.

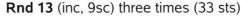

Head:

Starting at the nose

Ch2

Rnd 1 6sc in 2nd ch from the hook (6 sts)
Rnd 2 inc six times (12 sts)
Rnd 3 (3sc, inc) three times (15 sts)
Rnd 4 15sc (15 sts)
Rnd 5 1sc, inc, (4sc, inc) twice, 3sc (18 sts)
Rnd 6 18sc (18 sts)
Rnd 7 (5sc, inc) three times (21 sts)
Rnd 8 2sc, inc, (6sc, inc) twice, 4sc (24 sts)
Rnd 9–Rnd 10 24sc (24 sts)
Rnd 11 6sc, (inc, 3sc) three times, 6sc (27 sts)
Rnd 12 9sc, inc, (4sc, inc) twice, 7sc (30 sts)

Rnd 13 (inc, 9sc) three times (33 sts)
Rnd 14 6sc, inc, (10sc, inc) twice, 4sc (36 sts)
Rnd 15 1sc, dec, 15sc, inc, 2sc, inc, 12sc, dec (36 sts)
Rnd 16 36sc (36 sts)
Rnd 17 (5sc, inc) six times (42 sts)

Insert safety eyes between rounds 11 & 12. Start stuffing and continue adding more as you go.

Rnd 18–Rnd 19 42sc (42 sts)
Rnd 20 (5sc, dec) twice, 5sc, ch7, sk9, (5sc, dec) twice (29 + ch7sp sts)
Rnd 21 2sc, dec, 4sc, dec, 5sc, dec, 1sc in next 7ch, dec, 5sc, dec, 3sc (31 sts)
Rnd 22 (3sc, dec) twice, 2sc, dec, 2sc, sc3tog, 2sc, (dec, 3sc) twice (24 sts)
Rnd 23 (dec, 2sc) six times (18 sts)
Rnd 24 (1sc, dec) six times (12 sts)
Rnd 25 dec six times (6 sts)

Fasten off, leaving a piece of yarn for sewing.

Crest:

Join yarn to the first sc skipped in round 20, ch 1.

Rnd 1 Make 1sc in each of the skipped sts (9), inc in the side of sc (2), 1sc in each ch (7), inc in the side of sc (2) (20 sts)
Rnd 2–Rnd 3 20sc (20 sts)
Rnd 4 (4sc, dec) twice, 3sc, inc, 2sc, dec (18 sts)
Rnd 5 2sc, dec, 1sc, dec, 5sc, (inc, 2sc) twice (18 sts)
Rnd 6 (7sc, dec) twice (16 sts)
Rnd 7 16sc (16 sts)
Rnd 8 3sc, dec, 11sc (15 sts)
Rnd 9 (dec, 3sc) three times (12 sts)
Rnd 10 12sc (12 sts)

Start stuffing and continue adding more as you go.

Rnd 11 2sc, dec, 4sc, inc, 3sc (12 sts)

Rnd 12 1sc, sc3tog, 3sc, inc twice, 3sc
    (12 sts)
Rnd 13 dec three times, 6sc (9 sts)
Rnd 14 3sc, sc3tog twice (5 sts)

Fasten off, sew the opening closed.

Tail and body:

Starting at the tail

Ch2

Rnd 1 6sc in 2nd ch from the hook (6 sts)
Rnd 2 (1sc, inc) three times (9 sts)
Rnd 3 9sc (9 sts)
Rnd 4 (inc, 2sc) three times (12 sts)
Rnd 5–Rnd 6 12sc (12 sts)
Rnd 7 (inc, 3sc) three times (15 sts)
Rnd 8–Rnd 9 15sc (15 sts)
Rnd 10 (inc, 4sc) three times (18 sts)
Rnd 11–Rnd 13 18sc (18 sts)
Rnd 14 (inc, 5sc) three times (21 sts)
Rnd 15–Rnd 17 21sc (21 sts)
Rnd 18 9sc, inc, 1sc, inc, 9sc (23 sts)
Rnd 19 11sc, 3in1, 11sc (25 sts)
Rnd 20 2sc, (inc, 4sc) four times, inc, 2sc
    (30 sts)
Rnd 21 (inc, 4sc) six times (36 sts)
Rnd 22 36sc (36 sts)
Rnd 23 (11sc, inc) three times (39 sts)
Rnd 24 6sc, (inc, 12sc) twice, inc,
    6sc (42 sts)
Rnd 25 (13sc, inc) three times (45 sts)
Rnd 26–Rnd 37 45sc (45 sts)
Rnd 38 7sc, dec, (13sc, dec) twice,
    6sc (42 sts)
Rnd 39 42sc (42 sts)
Rnd 40 dec, 6sc, dec, 24sc, dec, 6sc (39 sts)
Rnd 41 3sc, dec, 5sc, dec, 23sc, dec, 2sc
    (36 sts)
Rnd 42 36sc (36 sts)

Start stuffing and continue adding more as
you go.

Rnd 43 (4sc, dec) twice, 12sc, (dec, 4sc)
    twice (32 sts)

Rnd 44 1sc, dec, (3sc, dec) twice, 6sc,
    (dec, 3sc) twice, dec, 1sc (26 sts)
Rnd 45 6sc, dec, 10sc, dec, 6sc (24 sts)
Rnd 46 dec, 2sc, dec, 14sc, dec, 2sc
    (21 sts)
Rnd 47 21sc (21 sts)
Rnd 48 dec, 19sc (20 sts)
Rnd 49 20sc (20 sts)

Rnd 50 1sc, dec, 15sc, dec (18 sts)
Rnd 51 6hdc, 8sc, 3hdc, 1sc (18 sts)

Fasten off, leaving a piece of yarn for sewing.

Back leg (make 2):
Starting at the foot

Ch2

Rnd 1 6sc in 2nd ch from the hook (6 sts)
Rnd 2 inc six times (12 sts)
Rnd 3 inc three times, 3in1, 1sc, 3in1,
     inc three times, 3sc (22 sts)
Rnd 4 3sc, inc, (5sc, inc) twice, 6sc (25 sts)
Rnd 5 6sc, 10hdc, 9sc (25 sts)
Rnd 6 25sc (25 sts)
Rnd 7 5sc, (dec, 2sc) four times, 4sc (21 sts)
Rnd 8 6sc, (dec, 1sc) three times, 6sc
     (18 sts)
Rnd 9 (1sc, dec) six times (12 sts)

Stuff the foot and continue adding more stuffing as you go.

Rnd 10–Rnd 11 12sc (12 sts)
Rnd 12 4sc, inc, 1sc, inc, 5sc (14 sts)
Rnd 13–Rnd 14 14sc (14 sts)
Rnd 15 (6sc, inc) twice (16 sts)
Rnd 16 (7sc, inc) twice (18 sts)
Rnd 17 (2sc, inc) six times (24 sts)
Rnd 18–Rnd 19 24sc (24 sts)
Rnd 20 (2sc, dec) six times (18 sts)
Rnd 21 (1sc, dec) six times (12 sts)
Rnd 22 dec six times (6 sts)

Fasten off, leaving a piece of yarn for sewing. Sew the opening closed.

Arm (make 2):
Starting at the "hand"

Ch2

Rnd 1 6sc in 2nd ch from the hook (6 sts)
Rnd 2 inc six times (12 sts)
Rnd 3 (3sc, inc) three times (15 sts)
Rnd 4–Rnd 6 15sc (15 sts)

Rnd 7 (dec, 1sc) three times, 6sc (12 sts)

Stuff the arm and continue adding more stuffing as you go.

Rnd 8–Rnd 15 12sc (12 sts)
Rnd 16 (2sc, dec) three times (9 sts)
Rnd 17 (1sc, dec) three times (6 sts)

Fasten off, leaving a piece of yarn for sewing. Sew the opening closed.

Assembling:

Attach the legs and arms on both sides of the body approx. between rounds 24 & 25 (back legs sts) and 43 & 44 (arms sts). If you want the legs to be movable, make sure that the yarn end is pulled out on the side of the leg, 1–2 rounds below the opening. Next, insert the needle in the body and through to the other side. Be careful to go between the stitches rather than through them. Take the other limb and run the needle through it. Then, insert the needle to the body exactly in the same place where it came from. Repeat with the yarn end from the other leg.

Sew the head to the body.

TIP
If you'd rather have the legs stationary and sewn under the belly, instead of on the sides, you can fasten off after round 16, stuff and attach them.